PREDESTINATION
MADE *EASY*

PREDESTINATION MADE *EASY*

New Edition

A Made *Easy* Series Book

Kenneth L. Gentry, Jr., Th.M., Th.D.

VICTORIOUS HOPE
PUBLISHING

Chesnee, South Carolina 29323
"Proclaiming the kingdom of God and teaching those things which
concern the Lord Jesus Christ, with all confidence."
(Acts 28:31)

Predestination Made Easy
New edition © 2020 by Gentry Family Trust udt April 2, 1999

The Made *Easy* Series from Victorious Hope Publishing provides substantial studies on significant issues in a succinct and accessible format from an evangelical and Reformed perspective.

Victorious Hope Publishing
P.O. Box 285
Chesnee, SC 29323

Printed in the United States of America

ISBN 978-1-7343620-0-8

Dedicated to

Ken Hall
A faithful Christian, strong Calvinist,
and good friend

TABLE OF CONTENTS

FOREWORD

There has always been doctrinal controversy in the Christian Church, whether over the nature of God in the early Trinitarian counsels, the divinity and humanity of Christ, or the doctrine of justification by faith as central and fundamental to the Reformation. Conflict concerning doctrine continues into this age, especially over the infallibility of the Holy Bible. However, of all the doctrinal controversies of the Church, none has been more heated, divisive, and emotional among Fundamentalists, Charismatics, Evangelicals, Reformed, and Liberals than the doctrine of "predestination."

Every Christian who truly believes the Bible is required to believe something about "predestination." Why? Because the term and concept are found in the Holy Scripture. It is therefore unavoidable that every Christian must study the doctrine as presented in the Bible. They must formulate some view on its meaning and purpose as determined by God, because He conveyed the concept to us in His Word. St. Paul wrote in Ephesians 1:4–5: "just as He chose us in Him before the foundation of the world, that we should be holy and without blame before Him, in love having predestined us to adoption as sons by Jesus Christ to Himself, according to the good pleasure of His will."

According to the Reformed theologian, Dr. Kenneth L. Gentry, Jr., the intellectual and historical development of this doctrine — along with all of its implications — need to be rightfully understood if one is going to ascertain God's ordained purpose in salvation. Too often this doctrine has been confused with the doctrine of "divine decrees," which deals with God's ordering of all things in the universe before creation. However, as Dr. Gentry points out, predestination deals primarily with the doctrine of the salvation of God's elect.

The fundamental understanding of this doctrine begins with a proper view concerning God himself. The question that arises is this: Can the decision concerning God's saving men be contingent upon anything outside of God Himself, such as the will of man? Since all things depend on God for their existence and meaning, should not this understanding also extend to the doctrine of salvation? When God chooses men for salvation, is not that determination based upon God's knowledge of His own will and exercised according to His good pleasure? And if so, how then can it be contingent upon the human exercise of the will? What does all this imply concerning the doctrine of predestination? And how does it relate to the issue of man's "free will"? These questions and many more are answered with great specificity by Dr. Gentry.

Predestination, as Dr. Gentry will point out, is the eternal act of God, whereby the future of every particular person in the human race has been determined beforehand by God. Whatever the individual wills or does, for good or for evil, is understood as performing a functional part, or outworking of God's ordained purpose. This applies to both the elect and the reprobate.

The doctrine of predestination is rooted in numerous Scriptures in the Old and New Testaments. It is especially found among the Epistles of Paul, and particularly in his Epistle to the Romans (chapter nine). Now all of this is to say that God has mercy on those whom He will have mercy and withholds mercy from those whom He will condemn for their sins. By God's grace, the elect are chosen by God and will be rescued from sin and the just penalty of death, the punishment due for sin (both original and actual). Predestination ensures that the elect shall dwell forever in God's presence. Those who are God's elect are sovereignly called by God the Father. They are regenerated through the work of the Holy Spirit, who gives the gift of faith which is the instrument whereby men are declared just based on the work of Jesus Christ alone. Those who are elect and justified will be sanctified and sealed by the Holy

Spirit until the day of redemption. This is the outworking of God's eternal Covenant. This is what God has promised those who were chosen in Christ Jesus before the foundation of the World.

In this book by Dr. Kenneth Gentry, the reader will be introduced to the doctrine of predestination in the context of the Scriptural meaning and purpose of a God who sovereignly saves individuals for His own glory. In addition, he will also demonstrate the many-faceted implications of this doctrine as it relates to Christianity. This book is a must read for all who call themselves Christian, whether they are pastors, students, or laymen, without regard to their denominational affiliation.

Kenneth Gary Talbot, Ph.D.
President
Whitefield College and Theological Seminary
Lakeland, Florida

Predestination is a big word, a deep concept, and a controversial doctrine. What is it all about?

Undoubtedly predestination is one of the most daunting, demanding, and debated doctrines in Scripture. As a Christian you certainly have heard of the doctrine, if for no other reason than because the word itself appears in the New Testament. In the beloved King James Version (KJV) "predestined" occurs four times: twice in Romans 8 (vv 29–30) and twice in Ephesians 1 (vv 5, 11). In the New American Standard Bible (NASB) it appears six times, in the Romans 8 and Ephesians 1 passages, as well as in Acts 4:28 and 1 Corinthians 2:7.

Your Bible says *something*, at least, about predestination. But what does it mean? If you have read any theological literature at all you surely have run into a wide range of statements regarding the deep and perplexing doctrine of predestination. You may even hold one of these views.

Predestination Teaching Denounced

Some denounce it as a "man-made doctrine," a "demonic theory," a "twisting of Scripture." Others deem predestination unbiblical, irrational, unjustifiable, unfair, immoral, and sadistic. Many will respond to any presentation of predestination by declaring: "My God wouldn't do that!" Or: "I refuse to worship such a God." Or "Surely the Bible doesn't teach fatalism!"

James Arminius declared that predestination "is repugnant to the Nature of God, but particularly to those Attributes of his nature by which he performs and manages all things, his wisdom, justice, and goodness."[1] Peter White cites one theologian who rejected predestination as "a most pernicious doctrine, and unfit for anyone to hear."[2] The famed Roman Catholic author, G. K. Chesterton (1874–1936), wrote about "that ancient heathen fatalism, which in the seventeenth century had taken the hardly less heathen form of Calvinism."[3]

One current Christian website declares that the doctrine is a "falsehood" which results from the "manipulation of Scripture" which leads to "the darkness of false doctrines." In calling it "the doctrine of devils," another site denounces it as "the most evil doctrine the devil ever came up with." Still another deems it "an unspeakably evil doctrine." And yet another website boldly declares:

> I believe it is the most evil doctrine ever invented by humankind. If it were true, religion, the Bible, our own lives, the entire creation would be pointless. It is all a game of a sadistic being who enjoys watching us suffer for his amusement. It is an insult to the very nature of a loving God. I can't see how anyone can believe in it and have any respect whatsoever for the divine.

And yet another site asserts: "One of the most horrible of all Christian heresies is that everyone's spiritual destiny has been predestined from the beginning of time — written as in a book of who will go to heaven and who will not."

Predestination Teaching Cautioned

Even strong predestination proponents recognize its difficulty. John Calvin (1509–64) can refer to certain aspects of the doctrine

---

[1] James Arminius, *The Words of Arminius* (vol. 1): "I Reject this Predestination for the Following Reasons: VII."

[2] Peter White, *Predestination, Policy and Polemic: Conflict and Consensus in the English Church from the Reformation to the Civil War* (Cambridge: University Press, 1992), 227.

[3] George L. Marlin, Richard P. Rabatin, and John L. Swan, *The Collection Works of G. K. Chesterton* (Ft. Collins, Colo.: Ignatius, 1991), 18:88.

by the Latin phrase *decretum horribilis* ("horrible decree"). By this he speaks of the terrifying prospect of predestination regarding the non-elect: their predestination to hell.

After defining the doctrine in powerful terms, the historic *Westminster Confession of Faith* (1646) calls predestination a "high mystery," declaring that "the doctrine of this high mystery of predestination is to be handled with special prudence and care" (WCF 3:8). The famed theologian Francis Turretin (1623–1687) cautions that "it should be taught soberly and prudently from the word of God so that two dangerous rocks may be avoided," recognizing that "there is a need here for great sobriety and prudence."

Predestination must not be treated cavalierly. But neither should we dismiss it due to its philosophical difficulty or man's emotional revulsion or Christians' widespread popular disdain. I will begin with a two-step *preparation* necessary before analyzing the doctrine, following Turretin's caution that "it ought not to be delivered immediately and in the first instance, but gradually and slowly." First, I will *define* predestination in terms of God's sovereignty (Ch. 2). Second, I will *discuss* the nature of God and his relationship to man (Ch. 3).

Then, and only then, will we be ready to begin investigating predestination itself (Chs. 4–10) — as it is revealed in Scripture and as it comes to practical expression in history.

Come, let us reason together!

Chapter 2
DEFINING THE CONCEPT

What do we mean by "predestination"?

Anytime we study a particular theological issue, we must insure that we understand precisely what we are studying. The more difficult the concept, the more likely it is to be confused, caricatured, and corrupted. In fact, both secularism's materialistic determinism and Islam's impersonalistic fatalism are often compared to biblical predestination, despite the fact that it fundamentally differs from them.

Consequently, I will begin by explaining what we mean not only by predestination, but by the interrelated ideas associated with it: God's ultimate sovereignty, general providence, and special election. Furthermore, we must be especially concerned how these matters inter-relate with and impact the biblical teaching on man's free will (or better: free moral agency) and his moral responsibility, as well as his real personality and genuine significance.

Ultimately by engaging these issues we are striving to understand the relationship of God and man, who are connected in the doctrine of predestination: God is the personal, loving, sovereign ruler, whereas man is the personal, covenant-obligated, ruled servant. All of these concepts are categorically, carefully, and clearly presented in the seventeenth century Reformed doctrinal statement called the *Westminster Confession of Faith* (WCF). I will be referring to this important theological document from time-to-time as a helpful tool for explaining predestination.

The view of predestination I will present is not simply my personal position on the subject. Rather, it is an historically approved, publicly verified, corporately affirmed, authoritatively declared doctrinal formulation found in the *Westminster Confession of Faith*. The doctrine found in the WCF is supported by other historic creeds and confessions, such as the Baptist Philadelphia Confession of Faith (1742). As I cite the relevant passages from the Confession I will italicize particularly relevant words and phrases.

WCF 2:2b: "He is the alone fountain of all being, of whom, through whom, and to whom are all things; and has *most sovereign dominion over them, to do by them, for them, or upon them whatsoever Himself pleases*. In His sight all things are open and manifest, His knowledge is infinite, infallible, and independent upon the creature, so as *nothing is to Him contingent, or uncertain*."

WCF 3:1: "God from *all eternity*, did, by the most wise and holy counsel of His own will, freely, and unchangeably ordain whatsoever comes to pass; yet so, as thereby neither is God the author of sin, nor is violence offered to the will of the creatures; nor is the liberty or contingency of second causes taken away, but rather established."

WCF 3:2: "Although God knows whatsoever may or can come to pass upon all supposed conditions; *yet has He not decreed anything because He foresaw it as future, or as that which would come to pass upon such conditions*."

WCF 3:3: "By the *decree of God*, for the manifestation of His glory, some men and angels are *predestinated unto everlasting life; and others foreordained to everlasting death*."

WCF 3:4: "These angels and men, *thus predestinated, and foreordained, are particularly and unchangeably designed*, and their number so certain and definite, that it cannot be either increased or diminished."

WCF 3:5: "Those of mankind that are *predestinated unto life*, God, *before the foundation of the world* was laid, according to

His eternal and immutable purpose, and the secret counsel and good pleasure of His will, has chosen, in Christ, unto everlasting glory, out of His mere free grace and love, *without any foresight of faith, or good works*, or perseverance in either of them, or any other thing in the creature, as conditions, or causes moving Him thereunto; and all to the praise of His glorious grace."

WCF 3:6: "As *God has appointed the elect unto glory*, so has He, *by the eternal and most free purpose of His will, foreordained all the means thereunto*. Wherefore, they who are *elected*, being fallen in Adam, are redeemed by Christ, are effectually called unto faith in Christ by His Spirit working in due season, are justified, adopted, sanctified, and kept by His power, through faith, unto salvation. Neither are any other redeemed by Christ, effectually called, justified, adopted, sanctified, and saved, but the elect only."

WCF 3:7: "The rest of mankind God was pleased, according to the unsearchable counsel of His own will, whereby He extends or withholds mercy, as He pleases, for the glory of His *sovereign power* over His creatures, to pass by; and *to ordain them to dishonor and wrath* for their sin, to the praise of His glorious justice."

WCF 3:8: "The doctrine of this high mystery of *predestination* is to be handled with special prudence and care, that men, attending the will of God revealed in His Word, and yielding obedience thereunto, may, from the certainty of their effectual vocation, be assured of their *eternal election*. So shall this doctrine afford matter of praise, reverence, and admiration of God; and of humility, diligence, and abundant consolation to all that sincerely obey the Gospel."

WCF 5:1: "God the great Creator of all things does *uphold, direct, dispose, and govern all creatures, actions, and things, from the greatest even to the least*, by His most wise and holy *providence*, according to His infallible foreknowledge, and the free and *immutable counsel of His own will*, to the praise of the glory of His wisdom, power, justice, goodness, and mercy."

WCF 5:2: "Although, in relation to the foreknowledge and decree of God, the first Cause, *all things come to pass immutably, and infallibly*; yet, by the same *providence*, He orders them to fall out, according to the nature of second causes, either necessarily, freely, or contingently."

WCF 5:3: "God, in His ordinary *providence*, makes use of means, yet is free to work without, above, and against them, at His pleasure."

WCF 5:4: "The almighty power, unsearchable wisdom, and infinite goodness of God so far manifest themselves in His *providence*, that it extends itself even to the first fall, and all other sins of angels and men; and that not by a bare permission, but such as has joined with it *a most wise and powerful bounding, and otherwise ordering, and governing of them*, in a manifold dispensation, to His own holy ends; yet so, as the sinfulness thereof proceeds only from the creature, and not from God, who, being most holy and righteous, neither is nor can be the author or approver of sin."

WCF 5:6: "As for those wicked and ungodly men whom God, as a righteous Judge, for former sins, does blind and harden, from them *He not only withholds His grace* whereby they might have been enlightened in their understandings, and wrought upon in their hearts; but sometimes also withdraws the gifts which they had, and exposes them to such objects as their corruption makes occasion of sin; and, withal, gives them over to their own lusts, the temptations of the world, and the power of Satan, whereby it comes to pass that they harden themselves, even under those means which God uses for the softening of others."

WCF 8:1: "It pleased God, in His *eternal purpose*, to *choose* and *ordain* the Lord Jesus, His only begotten Son, to be the Mediator between God and man, the Prophet, Priest, and King, the Head and Savior of His Church, the Heir of all things, and Judge of the world: unto whom *He did from all eternity give a people*, to be His seed, and to be by Him in time redeemed, called, justified, sanctified, and glorified."

WCF 8:6: "Although the work of redemption was not actually wrought by Christ till after His incarnation, yet the virtue, efficacy, and benefits thereof were communicated unto the *elect*, in all ages successively from the beginning of the world. . . ."

WCF 10:1: "*All those whom God hath predestinated unto life, and those only*, He is pleased, in His *appointed time*, effectually to call, by His Word and Spirit, out of that state of sin and death, in which they are by nature to grace and salvation, by Jesus Christ; enlightening their minds spiritually and savingly to understand the things of God, taking away their heart of stone, and giving unto them an heart of flesh; renewing their wills, and, by His *almighty power, determining them to that which is good*, and effectually drawing them to Jesus Christ: yet so, as they come most freely, being made willing by His grace."

WCF 10:2: "This effectual call is of God's free and special grace alone, *not from anything at all foreseen in man*, who is altogether passive therein, until, being quickened and renewed by the Holy Spirit, he is thereby enabled to answer this call, and to embrace the grace offered and conveyed in it."

WCF 10:4: "Others, *not elected*, although they may be called by the ministry of the Word, and may have some common operations of the Spirit, yet they never truly come unto Christ, and therefore cannot be saved. . . ."

WCF 11:4: "*God did, from all eternity, decree to justify all the elect*, and Christ did, in the fullness of time, die for their sins, and rise again for their justification: nevertheless, they are not justified, until the Holy Spirit does, in due time, actually apply Christ unto them."

WCF 17:2: "This perseverance of the saints depends not upon their own free will, but upon *the immutability of the decree of election*, flowing from the free and unchangeable love of God the Father. . . ."

WCF 21:1: "The light of nature shows that there is a God, who *has lordship and sovereignty over all*. . . ."

WCF 23:1: "God, the *supreme Lord* and King of all the world. . . ."

WCF 25:1: "The catholic or universal Church, which is invisible, consists of *the whole number of the elect*, that have been, are, or shall be gathered into one, under Christ the Head thereof. . . ."

As you can see, the Westminster Confession of Faith vigorously asserts the *absolute sovereignty of God*: It carefully distinguishes predestination from mere foreknowledge (prescience), conspicuously disassociates it from the actions of men (it is God's free action), categorically denies any fatalism (it is God's personal determination), and clearly secures it in eternity (it exists before time) even affirming *double predestination* (it covers the destiny of both the saved and the lost).

How are we to grasp such a bewildering doctrine? A doctrine that has caused such vigorous historical debate? A doctrine that seems so contrary to our own experience as free moral agents? A doctrine so offensive to the modern mind? Responding to these queries is the important task we have before us.

The Westminster Confession does not treat predestination naively; nor does it assert it arrogantly. Again please recall the Confession's caution: "The doctrine of this high mystery of predestination is to be handled with special prudence and care" (WCF 3:8). As indicated previously, part of our care in approaching the matter requires our understanding something about the parties involved in predestination (God and man) before we actually focus on the doctrine itself. Though most Christians would agree with what we are about to study, they do not keep such things in mind when approaching the "high mystery of predestination." Consequently, they recoil in confusion and horror at the concept.

The doctrine of predestination is a demanding doctrine. It is difficult for us to grasp both *intellectually* and *morally*. Intellectually, it perplexes our rationality as we try to comprehend it as a part of a broader, coherent, interrelated world-and-life view. Morally, it is alarming to affirm God's absolute sovereignty in light of man's moral perversity and the world's social condition. Our difficulty with predestination arises from the following biblical facts.

The Nature of God

We must begin by focusing on the nature of God himself, since predestination is a function of his mind and will, and controls all else.

God is infinite

Our primary problem in understanding predestination is that it starkly confronts us with the mind and ways of God. He is infinite in space (he is immense) and beyond time (he is eternal). To make matters more difficult still, he is holy (he is qualitatively perfect) in his whole being and all of his ways at all times. Thus, by the very nature of God's being, when confronting predestination we must sympathize with the country preacher who confessed: "We cannot unscrew the inscrutable."

In this regard, note once again the careful statements of the Confession:

> WCF 2:1a: "There is but one only, living, and true God, who is infinite in being and perfection, a most pure spirit, invisible, without body, parts, or passions; immutable, *immense, eternal, incomprehensible*, almighty, *most wise, most holy, most free, most absolute*; working all things according to the counsel of His own immutable and most righteous will, for His own glory."

> WCF 7:1: "The *distance between God and the creature is go great*, that although reasonable creatures do owe obedience unto Him as their Creator, yet they could never have any fruition of Him as their blessedness and reward, but by some voluntary condescension on God's part, which He has been pleased to express by way of covenant."

> WCF 16:5: This paragraph speaks of "the *infinite distance* that is between us and God."

So then, God is not simply larger and more powerful than us, as a quantitative matter. He is not only *quantitatively* (infinitely!) more vast, but *qualitatively* different. This is because God exists in the eternal realm beyond our direct experience and our intellectual comprehension.

In terms of his spatial immensity, God is beyond any space limitations such as constrain us. Consequently, he is beyond our capacity to fully conceive his absolute being. He is not simply quantitatively immense, as is Mt. Everest, which looms over us in the world; nor even as the unspeakably enormous Universe itself, which contains around 125 billion galaxies each containing hundreds of millions of stars. The immensity of God is even more remarkable still. He is *infinite* in his being, without any limit or end.[1] He is not confined by the limits even of the Universe, which some astronomers believe to be 156 billion light-years across.[2]

> Can you discover the depths of God? / Can you discover the limits of the Almighty? / They are high as the heavens, what can you do? / Deeper than Sheol, what can you know? / Its measure is longer than the earth / And broader than the sea. (Job 11:7–9)

> Will God indeed dwell on the earth? Behold, heaven and the highest heaven cannot contain Thee. (1 Kgs 8:27)

> Where can I go from Your Spirit? Or where can I flee from Your presence? If I ascend to heaven, You are there; If I make my bed in Sheol, behold, You are there. If I take the wings of the dawn, if I dwell in the remotest part of the sea, even there Your hand will lead me, and Your right hand will lay hold of me. (Psa 139:7–10)

> "Can a man hide himself in hiding places / So I do not see him?" declares the LORD. / "Do I not fill the heavens and the earth?" declares the LORD.

What is more, his *entire indivisible essence* is at *every moment* of time *present in its fullness* in *every point of space* throughout the Uni-

-----

[1] The etymology of the word "infinite" is derived from compounding two Latin words: *in* is a prefix having a negative force, similar to our "un." *Finite* is from *finire* (from which we derive our word "finish"), and means "to stop or limit." Thus, "infinite" means unlimited, unmeasurable, unbounded, endless.

[2] A light-year is 5,878,625,373,183 miles (the distance light travels in one year). Thus, with a light-year being (approximately) 6 trillion miles, the Universe is somewhere in the neighborhood of 936 billion-trillion miles across. Or to put it another way, it is 936 sextillion miles across, which is 936 followed by twenty-one zeroes. This prodigious figure is even daunting to comedian Stephen Wright who believes "anyplace is walking distance if you have the time."

verse. Thus we read that the "eyes of the Lord are in every place" (Prov 15:3; cp. 2 Chron. 16:9; Jer. 16:17; Zech. 4:10).[3] Consequently, there is "no creature hidden from His sight, but all things are naked and open to the eyes of Him" (Heb 4:13; cp. Psa. 11:4; 33:13–15).

God is also beyond any time limitations such as we experience. He never had a beginning and will never have an end. Though he governs us by determining our time on earth (Gen 1:14–16; Acts 17:26) and teaching us to number our days (Psa. 90:12; cp. Job 14:5; Psa. 39:4), he is himself beyond and above time. Furthermore, as an eternal being his thoughts and purposes are eternal and without succession, being one and inseparable forever.[4] He never learns anything new, nor forgets anything he currently knows.

> For thus says the High and exalted One / Who lives forever, whose name is Holy. (Isa 57:15a)

> Behold, God is exalted, and we do not know Him; / The number of His years is unsearchable. (Job 36:26)

> Before the mountains were born / Or You gave birth to the earth and the world, / Even from everlasting to everlasting, You are God. (Psa 90:2)

> "I am the Alpha and the Omega," says the Lord God, "who is and who was and who is to come, the Almighty." (Rev 1:8)

God is independent

Unlike us, God is absolutely independent. He exists in and of himself without reference to or dependence upon anything else. He is absolute, self-existent, and the very ground of all being. We are dependent beings: the cause of our being and our continued exis-

---

[3] See: A. A. Hodge, *Outlines of Theology* (Edinburgh: Banner of Truth, rep. 1878), 140.

[4] Hodge, *Outlines of Theology*, 143.

tence lies outside of ourselves. As the Confession of Faith expresses it:

> God has all life, glory, goodness, blessedness, *in and of Himself*; and *is alone in and unto Himself all-sufficient*, not standing in need of any creatures which He has made, nor deriving any glory from them, but only manifesting His own glory in, by, unto, and upon them. He is the alone fountain of all being, of whom, through whom, and to whom are all things; and has most sovereign dominion over them, to do by them, for them, or upon them whatsoever Himself pleases. In His sight all things are open and manifest, *His knowledge is infinite, infallible, and independent upon the creature, so as nothing is to Him contingent, or uncertain.* (WCF 2:2)

God reveals himself to Moses with the powerful statement in Exodus 3:14: "And God said to Moses, 'I AM WHO I AM.'" This speaks of our Creator in terms of his eternal self-sufficiency, quite unlike our experience as time-bound and physically-dependent creatures. The Bible clearly presents and constantly maintains the fundamental distinction between God and man, affirming the foundational Creator/creature distinction. As I will reiterate from throughout this study, Bible-based theology holds to a two-level reality: God and all else, the Creator and the creation (Rom 1:25). Thus, Scripture appropriately opens with the profound assertion: "In the beginning God created the heavens and the earth" (Gen 1:1). This distinguishes God and creation, showing him already existing when all else begins to be created.

This two-level reality is emphasized in numerous Scriptures, as we see from the following samples.

> Do you not know? Have you not heard? / Has it not been declared to you from the beginning? / Have you not understood from the foundations of the earth? / It is He who sits above the vault of the earth, / And its inhabitants are like grasshoppers, / Who stretches out the heavens like a curtain / And spreads them

out like a tent to dwell in. / He it is who reduces rulers to nothing, / Who makes the judges of the earth meaningless. / Scarcely have they been planted, / Scarcely have they been sown, / Scarcely has their stock taken root in the earth, / But He merely blows on them, and they wither, / And the storm carries them away like stubble. / 'To whom then will you liken Me / That I should be his equal?' says the Holy One. / Lift up your eyes on high / And see who has created these stars, / The One who leads forth their host by number, / He calls them all by name; / Because of the greatness of His might and the strength of His power / Not one of them is missing. (Isa 40:21–26)

The Father has life in Himself. (John 5:26a)

Neither is He served by human hands, as though He needed anything, since He Himself gives to all life and breath and all things. (Acts 17:25)

God is perfect

God is absolutely perfect in his being and all his knowledge, wisdom, will, and ways. He is absolutely free from all defect; no imperfection mars him or threatens to confuse him. He exists in absolute majestic excellence and is the standard of perfection, lacking nothing that is desirable.

God is not a man, that He should lie, / Nor a son of man, that He should repent; / Has He said, and will He not do it? / Or has He spoken, and will He not make it good? (Num 23:19)

The Rock! His work is perfect, / For all His ways are just; / A God of faithfulness and without injustice, / Righteous and upright is He. (Deut 32:4)

As for God, His way is blameless; / The word of the Lord is tried; / He is a shield to all who take refuge in Him. (Psa 18:30)

For I, the Lord, do not change; therefore you, O sons of Jacob, are not consumed. (Mal 3:6)

Your heavenly Father is perfect. (Matt 5:48)

In him there is no variation, or shifting shadow. (Jms 1:18b)

As we have seen, God is infinite, eternal, independent, and perfect. He is truly magnificent and all glorious. He is distinct from all
else in the Universe, and therefore wholly unique. Keeping these
truths in mind, let us now consider the other part of the predestination equation, by focusing on:

The Nature of Man

Having briefly summarized the majesty of God, we must now
remind ourselves of the smallness and imperfection of man. All of
this will be important for recognizing why we are overwhelmed by
the doctrine of God's absolute sovereignty in predestination.

All evangelical *Christians* agree on the fundamental difference
between God and man; this is not peculiar to any predestinarian
theology.[5] Nevertheless, in order to carefully approach the matter
of predestination, we must build up our fuller doctrinal system
from well-known, foundational issues — such as man's creaturely
status as a finite and temporal being, as well as his fallen, sinful
condition.

As careful Christians we must draw in a wide sampling of biblical doctrine before leaping to theological conclusions on any particular issue. Scripture presents a unified *system* of belief, not a dis-
orderly *collection* of claims. The issues regarding man as understood
over against God are setting the stage for an important first point
in the debate over predestination (as we shall see).

---

[5] However, it is different from Mormonism which teaches that God was once
a man and that Mormons shall become gods. Their famous couplet summarizes
this horrendous theology: "As man is, God once was. As God is, man may
become." This was declared by Lorenzo Snow, the first President of the Church
of Jesus Christ, Latter-day saints.

Doctrinal study should not be a matter of intellectual pride before men, but a means to deeper devotion to God. Study of God's Word is designed to "sanctify" us (John 17:17; Heb 5:12–14), not make us arrogant (1 Cor 8:1) or quarrelsome (2 Tim 2:24). We should never be guilty of "itching ears" (2 Tim 4:3) for:

> the *goal of our instruction* is love from a pure heart and a good conscience and a sincere faith. For some men, straying from these things, have turned aside to *fruitless discussion*, wanting to be teachers of the Law, even though they do not understand either what they are saying or the matters about which they make confident assertions. (1 Tim 1:5–7)

The Confession carefully presents man's nature by noting that "the *distance between God and the creature is go great*" (WCF 7:1). It also presents our fallen, sinful condition in no uncertain terms.

> WCF 5:4: The *sinfulness thereof proceeds only from the creature*, and not from God, who, being most holy and righteous, neither is nor can be the author or approver of sin.

> WCF 6:1: Our first parents, being seduced by the subtilty and temptations of Satan, *sinned*, in eating the forbidden fruit. This their sin, God was pleased, according to His wise and holy counsel, to permit, having purposed to order it to His own glory.

> WCF 6:2: *By this sin they fell from their original righteousness* and communion, with God, and so became *dead in sin*, and *wholly defiled* in all the parts and faculties of soul and body.

> WCF 6:3: They being the root of all mankind, the guilt of this sin was imputed; and the same death in sin, and *corrupted nature*, conveyed to all their posterity descending from them by ordinary generation.

> WCF 6:4: From this original corruption, whereby we *are utterly indisposed, disabled, and made opposite to all good*, and *wholly inclined to all evil*, do proceed all actual transgressions.

WCF 7:3: Man, by his fall, having made himself *incapable of life* by that covenant. . . .

WCF 9:3: Man, by his fall into a state of sin, has *wholly lost all ability of will to any spiritual good* accompanying salvation: so as, a natural man, being *altogether averse from that good, and dead in sin, is not able,* by his own strength, to convert himself, or to prepare himself thereunto.

WCF 15:2: Of the *filthiness* and *odiousness of his sins,* as contrary to the holy nature, and righteous law of God. . . .

WCF 16:5: We cannot by our best works merit pardon of sin, or eternal life at the hand of God, by reason of the *great disproportion* that is between them and the glory to come; and the *infinite distance that is between us and God,* whom, by them, we can neither profit, nor satisfy for the debt of our former sins, but when we have done all we can, we have done but our duty, and are unprofitable servants: and because, as they are good, they proceed from His Spirit, and as they are wrought by us, they are defiled, and mixed with so much *weakness* and *imperfection,* that they *cannot endure the severity of God's judgment.*

WCF 19:6: The *sinful pollutions* of their nature, hearts and lives."

But we want to be *biblical* theologians. So let us consider the Scripture revelation regarding these matters.

Man is finite

Man is limited in his being and power, and is infinitesimally small compared even to his physical environment — not only the planet we live on but ultimately the entire Universe. And when compared to God himself, he is less than nothing.

Then the Lord answered Job out of the whirlwind and said, "Who is this that darkens counsel / By words without knowledge? / Now gird up your loins like a man, / And I will ask you, and you instruct Me! / *Where were you when I laid the foundation of the earth?*

/ Tell Me, if you have understanding, / Who set its measurements, since you know? / Or who stretched the line on it?" (Job 38:15)

Then the Lord said to Job, "Will the faultfinder contend with the Almighty? / Let him who reproves God answer it." / Then Job answered the Lord and said, / "Behold, *I am insignificant*; what can I reply to You? / I lay my hand on my mouth."[6] (Job 40:1–4)

Behold, *the nations are like a drop from a bucket,* a And are regarded as a *speck of dust on the scales*; / Behold, He lifts up the islands like fine dust. / Even Lebanon is not enough to burn, / Nor its beasts enough for a burnt offering. *All the nations are as nothing before Him*, they are regarded by Him as *less than nothing and meaningless.* (Isa 40:15–17)

On the contrary, who are you, O man, who answers back to God? The thing molded will not say to the molder, "Why did you make me like this," will it? (Rom 9:20)

Man is temporal

Though man is created in the image of God (Gen 1:26; 9:6; Col 4:10) and can do marvelous things, he is limited by time constraints.[7] Such constraints curtail our ability to comprehend the enormity of the world and of the Universe. We simply do not have enough time to fully engage study of all the things of God.

Man, who is born of woman, / is *short-lived* and full of turmoil. / Like a flower *he comes forth and withers.* / He also *flees like a shadow and does not remain.* . . . / Since his *days are determined,* / the number of his months is with You, / And *his limits Thou hast set* so that he cannot pass. (Job 14: 1–2, 5)

---

[6] Read Job 38–41 for a detailed response of God to Job on this matter; read Isaiah 40 for a glorious description of God's majesty.

[7] Even earliest man quickly developed culture, include raising livestock, creating music and musical instruments, and making metal tools and implements (Gen 4:21–22). See Kenneth L. Gentry, Jr., *The Greatness of the Great Commission: The Christian Enterprise in a Fallen World* (Chesnee, S.C.: Victorious Hope, 1993), ch. 1.

You turn man back into dust / And say, "Return, O children of men." / For a thousand years in Your sight / Are like yesterday when it passes by, / Or as a watch in the night. / You have swept them away like a flood, they fall asleep; / In the morning they are like grass which sprouts anew. / In the morning it flourishes and sprouts anew; / Toward evening it fades and withers away. (Psa 90:3–6)

As for man, his days are like grass; / As a flower of the field, so he flourishes. (Psa 103:15)

The grass withers, the flower fades, / When the breath of the Lord blows upon it; / Surely *the people are grass*. (Isa 40:7)

What is your life? It is even a vapor that appears for a little time and then vanishes away. (Jms 4:14b)

Man is fallen

Reformed (Calvinistic) theology has a much stronger conception of sin's enormity than non-Reformed theologies. This is partially due to its higher conception of God himself (from which predestination flows!). But it is also based on a deep commitment to the Word of God, even when it startles or overwhelms us.

Reformed theology holds to the "total depravity" of man. This doctrine not only teaches that all men are sinners from their conception, but highlights the depth and pervasiveness of sin. Sin affects *every* aspect of man's being — not only his will, emotions, desires, and strength, but even his intellect. As Konstantinovsky expresses it: depravity "is a condition characterized by a universal inbred aversion to virtue, a disposition toward vice, and a departure from the resemblance to the divine prototype."[8]

This doctrine does not imply that man is as evil as he can be, for God's common grace prevents the absolute dominion of sin while

---

[8] Julia Konstantinovsky in Christopher M. Hays, *When the Son of Man Didn't Come* (Philadelphia: Fortress, 2016), 124.

he lives on earth. Only in hell, when God's common grace is finally removed, will men be purely evil.

All men are sinners. Men are *not* inherently good, nor are they born in a "neutral" condition:

> There is no one who does not sin. (2 Chr 6:36b; cp. 1Kgs 8:46)

> If You, LORD, should mark iniquities, O Lord, who could stand? (Psa 130:3)

> In Your sight no man living is righteous. (Psa 143:2b)

> Indeed, there is not a righteous man on earth who continually does good and who never sins. (Eccl 7:20)

> There is none who understands; There is none who seeks after God. . . . For all have sinned and fall short of the glory of God. (Rom 3:11, 23)

> Wherefore, as by one man sin entered into the world, and death by sin; and so death passed upon all men, for that all have sinned. (Rom 5:12)

> If we say that we have no sin, we are deceiving ourselves, and the truth is not in us. . . . If we say that we have not sinned, we make Him a liar, and His word is not in us. (1 John 1:8, 10)

The Scripture clearly notes man's inherently fallen condition as the source of his moral turpitude — even from the moment of conception. As natural-born sinners, we have an internal proclivity to rebel against God:

> The intent of man's heart is *evil from his youth*. (Gen 8:21c)

> What is man, that he should be pure, or he who is born of a woman, that he should be righteous? (Job 14:14)

> Behold, I was brought forth in iniquity, and in sin my mother *conceived* me. (Psa 51:5)

The wicked are *estranged from the womb*; these who speak lies go astray from birth. (Psa 58:3)

We [who are now Christians] all once conducted ourselves in the lusts of our flesh, fulfilling the desires of the flesh and of the mind, and were by *nature* children of wrath, just as the others. (Eph 2:3)

Our whole nature is corrupted by sin so that we are depraved in every aspect of our being. Sin is not a sickness that hinders us intermittently; it is a foul death corrupting us permanently. As Paul expresses it, we are *"dead* in trespasses and sins" so that outside of Christ we are subject to "the prince of the power of the air" (Satan) and are actually "sons of disobedience" (Eph 2:1–2).

We are depraved in *heart* and moral tendencies (Jer 17:9; John 3:19) and *will* (John 5:40; 6:44; Jer 13:23; Matt 7:18). But especially for our concern with understanding predestination, we must note that our *mind* and *thinking processes* are also fallen and corrupted:

This I say therefore, and affirm together with the Lord, that you walk no longer just as the Gentiles also walk, in the *futility of their mind, being darkened in their understanding*, excluded from the life of God, because of the *ignorance that is in them*, because of the hardness of their heart; and they, having become callous, have given themselves over to sensuality, for the practice of every kind of impurity with greediness. (Eph 4:17–19)

For the wrath of God is revealed from heaven against all ungodliness and unrighteousness of men, who suppress the truth in unrighteousness. (Rom 1:18)

Because the carnal *mind* is enmity against God; for it is not subject to the law of God, nor indeed can be. (Rom 8:7)

Sin affects our notion of self, rights, values, obligations, morality, and more. Indeed, it alters our entire outlook on the world and God himself. Our impairment regarding these issues will make it naturally difficult for us to understanding and accept some of the hard doctrines of Scripture.

The Mystery in God

As we gather together the above biblical material, we must realize that our finite, temporal, fallen condition will greatly encumber our ability to understand the infinite, eternal, perfect Creator. How could it be otherwise? Therefore, our strong biblically-based, Christian worldview actually *expects* "mystery" in contemplating God and his ways. If we could fully and easily comprehend him, he would be less than he reveals himself to be and less than our theology expects.

This conclusion should prepare us to be overwhelmed when we try to comprehend his eternal plan. With Paul, in the end we must "let God be true and every man a liar" (Rom 3:4). With Job we must ultimately declare: "Behold, I am insignificant; what can I reply to Thee? / I lay my hand on my mouth. / Once I have spoken, and I will not answer; / Even twice, and I will add no more" (Job 40:4–5).

But our recognizing mystery in God is not just a theological *implication*. It is actually an exegetical *observation* drawn from clear and direct revelation in Scripture.

> God does great and unsearchable things, wonders without number. (Job 5:9)

> Can you discover the depths of God? / Can you discover the limits of the Almighty? (Job 11:7)

> Do you hear the secret counsel of God, / And limit wisdom to yourself? (Job 15:8)

> God thunders with His voice wondrously, / Doing great things which we cannot comprehend. (Job 37:5)

> Then Job answered the LORD and said, "I know that You can do all things, / And that no purpose of Yours can be thwarted. / Who

is this that hides counsel without knowledge? / Therefore I have declared that which I did not understand, / Things too wonderful for me, which I did not know. / 'Hear, now, and I will speak; / I will ask You, and You instruct me.'" (Job 42:1–4)

For as high as the heavens are above the earth, / So great is His lovingkindness toward those who fear Him. (Psa 103:11)

Such knowledge is too wonderful for me; it is too high, I cannot attain to it. (Psa 139:6)

Who has directed the Spirit of the LORD, / as His counselor has informed Him? With whom did He consult and who gave Him understanding? / And who taught Him in the path of justice and taught Him knowledge / And informed Him of the way of understanding? Behold, the nations are like a drop from a bucket, / And are regarded as a speck of dust on the scales; / Behold, He lifts up the islands like fine dust.... / Do you not know? Have you not heard? / The Everlasting God, the LORD, the Creator of the ends of the earth /Does not become weary or tired. / His understanding is inscrutable. (Isa 40:13–15, 28d)

"For My thoughts are not your thoughts, / Neither are your ways My ways," declares the Lord. / "For as the heavens are higher than the earth, / So are My ways higher than your ways, / And My thoughts than your thoughts. / For as the rain and the snow come down from heaven, / And do not return there without watering the earth, / And making it bear and sprout, / And furnishing seed to the sower and bread to the eater; / So shall My word be which goes forth from My mouth; / It shall not return to Me empty, / Without accomplishing what I desire, / And without succeeding in the matter for which I sent it." (Isa 55:8–11)

O the depth of the riches both of the wisdom and knowledge of God! how unsearchable are his judgments, and his ways past finding out! For who hath known the mind of the Lord? or who hath been his counsellor? Or who hath first given to him, and it shall be recompensed unto him again? (Rom 11:33–35)

For who has known the mind of the Lord, that he should instruct Him? But we have the mind of Christ. (1 Cor 2:16)

To me, the very least of all saints, this grace was given, to preach to the Gentiles the unfathomable riches of Christ. . . . in order that the manifold wisdom of God might now be made known through the church to the rulers and the authorities in the heavenly places. (Eph 3:8, 10)

Conclusion

Since we will be contemplating the challenging doctrine of pre-destination, we have to approach the matter carefully. In this chapter I have briefly presented the nature of the one who predestines (God) as well as of the one who is predestined (man). Our study shows that if we seriously reflect on God, we will be overwhelmed by his infinite, eternal, perfect being. Such a study of God becomes all the more remarkable when we realize our own circumstances and condition as finite, temporal, fallen creatures.

A proper understanding of the doctrine of God and the doctrine of man leads us to expect mystery in the person and ways of God. This is exactly what we experience when we study the perplexing doctrine of predestination. Unfortunately, too many Christians do not carefully consider these matters when they hastily dismiss the doctrine as both incomprehensible and reprehensible.

But now we are ready to look to the Scriptures for the *proof* of predestination. We must ask, as Jesus often did of his opponents: "Have you not read?" (Matt 12:3, 5; 19:4; 22:31; Mark 12:10, 26).

Chapter 4
DEMONSTRATING ITS SCRIPTURALNESS

In the previous chapters I was *indirectly* showing that the litmus test of a doctrine's validity is its scripturalness. We must seek in Scripture a "thus saith the Lord!" Having warned against mere emotional revulsion or intellectual recoil at the doctrine of predestination, I must now urge the adopting of the noble Berean spirit: "Now these were more noble- minded than those in Thessalonica, for they received the word with great eagerness, examining the Scriptures daily, to see whether these things were so" (Acts 17:11). Thus, we must hear Isaiah's call: "To the law and to the testimony! If they do not speak according to this word, it is because they have no light" (Isa 8:20). We should accept Christ's challenge to the Pharisees to "search the Scriptures" (John 5:39).

When Paul declares the gospel to the Jews he necessarily reasons with them *from Scripture*: "And according to *Paul's custom*, he went to them, and for three Sabbaths *reasoned with them from the Scriptures*" (Acts 17:2). "And they came to Ephesus, and he left them there. Now he himself entered the synagogue and reasoned with the Jews . . . for he powerfully refuted the Jews in public, demonstrating by the Scriptures that Jesus was the Christ" (Acts 18:19, 28). When we reason within ourselves and with our fellow Christians about the doctrine of predestination, we too must reason from Scripture rather than from emotion.

The *Westminster Confession of Faith* notes that "the doctrine of this high mystery of predestination is to be handled with special prudence and care" (WCF 3:8). By offering all the previous preparation, we are approaching the matter very carefully. We are now at a vitally important juncture in our study. Since we are contemplating predestination, only now are we ready to speak directly to the matter. The next step should by itself be compelling to the Christian who accepts the previous line of reasoning.

As our *first* step in our *biblical* (as opposed to our methodological) argument, we will simply pile on the Scripture passages emphasizing predestination. We will avoid all explication of the texts at this point. As we will see, the Scripture repeatedly speaks of the absolute sovereignty of God from a variety of angles and employing various terms, including election, predestination, foreordination, choosing, predetermination, counsel, and purpose. These are abundantly affirmed in Scripture, oftentimes using one of these words themselves, but sometimes clearly assuming the concept apart from the express terms.

Of course, the best method here is to cite those verses which are most direct and clear. So at this point I will simply cite one verse after another, organizing them into general categories. I will not record every relevant verse in Scripture (there are too many!), but I will demonstrate the overwhelming evidence for predestination in God's word. Too often, protests against predestination arise from an unfamiliarity with the biblical evidence. A survey of some of the abundant evidence will belie the claim that predestination is alien to Scripture, alerting the Christian to very real presence of the doctrine in Scripture.

God's Absolute Sovereignty

But indeed for this purpose I have raised you up, that I may show My power in you, and that My name may be declared in all the earth. (Exo 9:16)

And he said, "I will make all my goodness pass before thee, and I will proclaim the name of the LORD before thee; and *will be gracious to whom I will be gracious*, and *will shew mercy on whom I will shew mercy*." (Exo 33:19)

For it was of the LORD to harden their hearts, that they should come against Israel in battle, *that he might destroy them utterly*, and that they might have no favour, but that he might destroy them, as the LORD commanded Moses. (Josh 11:20)

Then Job answered the Lord, and said, / "I know that *Thou canst do all things*, / and that *no purpose of Thine can be thwarted*." (Job 42:1–2)

Our God is in the heavens; / He does *whatever He pleases*. (Psa 115:3)

Whatever the Lord pleases, He does, / In heaven and in earth, in the seas and in all deeps. (Psa 135:6)

The LORD hath *made all things for himself*: yea, even the wicked for the day of evil. (Prov 16:4 KJV)

In his heart a man plans his course, but *the Lord determines his steps*. (Prov 16:9)

The Lord of hosts has sworn saying, "Surely, *just as I have intended so it has happened*, and just as I have planned so it will stand, for the Lord of hosts has planned, and who can frustrate it? And as for His stretched-out hand, who can turn it back?" (Isa 14:24, 27)

And who is like Me? Let him proclaim and declare it; / Yes, let him recount it to Me in order, / From the time that I established the ancient nation. / And let them declare to them the things that are coming / And the events that are going to take place. (Isa 44:7)

Declaring the end from the beginning / And from ancient times things which have not been done, / Saying, "My purpose will be established, / And I will accomplish all My good pleasure; / Calling a bird of prey from the east, / The man of My purpose from a far country. / Truly I have spoken; truly I will bring it to pass. / I have planned it, surely I will do it." (Isa 46:10–11)

Now the word of the Lord came to me saying, / Before I formed you in the womb I knew you, / And before you were born I consecrated you; / I have appointed you a prophet to the nations. (Jer 1:4–5)

If a trumpet is blown in a city will not the people tremble? / If a calamity occurs in a city has not the Lord done it? (Amos 3:6)

At that time Jesus answered and said, "I thank you, O Father, Lord of heaven and earth, because *you hid these things* from the wise and prudent, and have revealed them unto babes. Even so, Father: for so it seemed good in Your sight." (Matt 11:25–26)

Then shall the King say unto them on his right hand, "Come, ye blessed of my Father, inherit the kingdom prepared for you *from the foundation of the world*." (Matt 25:34)

And he said, "Unto you it is given to know the mysteries of the kingdom of God: but to others in parables; that seeing they might not see, and *hearing they might not understand*." (Luke 8:10)

Him, being delivered by the *determinate counsel and foreknowledge of God*, ye have taken, and by wicked hands have crucified and slain. (Acts 2:23)

For truly in this city there were gathered together against Your holy servant Jesus, whom You anointed, both Herod and Pontius Pilate, along with the Gentiles and the peoples of Israel, to *do whatever Your hand and Your purpose predestined to occur*. (Acts 4:27–28)

And [God] hath made of one blood all nations of men for to dwell on all the face of the earth, and hath *determined the times before appointed*, and the bounds of their habitation. (Acts 17:26)

But *when it pleased God*, who separated me from my mother's womb, and *called* me by his grace. . . . (Gal 1:15)

For we are His workmanship, created in Christ for good works, which God *prepared before hand* that we should walk in them. (Eph 2:10)

Who verily was *foreordained before the foundation of the world*, but was manifest in these last times for you. (1 Pet 1:20)

God's Sovereign Calling

And God said unto Abraham, Let it not be grievous in your sight because of the lad, and because of your bondwoman; in all that Sarah has said unto you, hearken unto her voice; for *in Isaac shall your seed be called*. (Gen 21:12–13)

For You are an holy people unto the LORD your God: the LORD your God has *chosen* you to be a special people unto himself, above all people that are upon the face of the earth. The LORD did not *set his love upon you*, nor *choose* you, because you were more in number than any people; for you were the fewest of all people: But because the LORD loved you, and because he would keep the oath which he had sworn unto your fathers, has the LORD brought you out with a mighty hand, and redeemed you out of the house of bondmen, from the hand of Pharaoh king of Egypt. (Deut 7:6–8)

Blessed is the nation whose God is the LORD, / The people whom he has *chosen* for his own inheritance. (Psa 33:12)

How blessed is the one whom You choose, and bring near to Thee, / To dwell in Your courts. / We will be satisfied with the goodness of Your house, / Your holy temple. (Psa 65:4)

All things have been handed over to Me by My Father; and no one knows the Son, except the Father; nor does anyone know the Father, except the Son, and *anyone to whom the Son wills to reveal Him*. (Matt 11:27)

So the last shall be first, and the first last: for many be called, but *few chosen*. (Matt 20:16)

Shall not God bring about justice for His *elect*, who cry to Him day and night, and will He delay long over them? (Luke 18:7)

All that the Father *gives Me* will come to Me, and the one who comes to Me I will by no means cast out. (John 6:37)

And this is the Father's will which hath sent me, that of all which he hath *given* me I should lose nothing, but should raise it up again at the last day. (John 6:39)

No man can come to me, except the Father which hath sent me *draw* him: and I will raise him up at the last day. (John 6:44)

I speak not of you all: I know whom I have *chosen*: but that the scripture may be fulfilled, He that eateth bread with me hath lifted up his heel against me. (John 13:18)

You did not choose Me, but I chose you and appointed you that you should go and bear fruit. (John 15:16a)

If ye were of the world, the world would love his own: but because ye are not of the world, but I have *chosen* you out of the world, therefore the world hateth you. (John 15:19)

Jesus spoke these words, lifted up His eyes to heaven, and said: Father, the hour has come. Glorify Your Son, that Your Son also may glorify You, as You have given Him authority over all flesh, that *He should give eternal life to as many as You have given Him.* (John 17:1–2)

I have manifested Your name unto the men whom *You gave me* out of the world: Yours they were, and You gave them me; and they have kept Your word. . . . I pray for them: I pray not for the world, but for them which *You have given me*; for they are Yours. (John 17:6, 9)

For the promise is unto you, and to your children, and to all that are afar off, even *as many as the Lord our God shall call.* (Acts 2:39)

Now when the Gentiles heard this, they were glad and glorified the word of the Lord. And *as many as had been appointed to eternal life believed.* (Acts 13:48)

And he said, "The God of our fathers has *chosen* you, that you should know his will, and see that Just One, and should hear the voice of his mouth." (Acts 22:14)

(For the children not yet being born, nor having done any good or evil, that the purpose of God according to election might stand, not of works but of Him who calls), it was said to her, "The older shall serve the younger." As it is written, "Jacob I have loved, but Esau I have hated." What shall we say then? Is there unrighteousness with God? Certainly not! For He says to Moses, "*I will have mercy on whomever I will have mercy, and I will have compassion on whomever I will have compassion.*" So then it is not of him who wills, nor of him who runs, but of God who shows mercy. For the Scripture says to Pharaoh, "For this very purpose I have raised you up, that I may show My power in you, and that My name may be declared in all the earth." Therefore *He has mercy on whom He wills, and whom He wills He hardens.* You will say to me then, "Why does He still find fault? For who has resisted His will?" But indeed, O man, who are you to reply against God? Will the thing formed say to him who formed it, "Why have you made me like this?" *Does not the potter have power over the clay, from the same lump to make one vessel for honor and another for dishonor?* What if God, wanting to show His wrath and to make His power known, endured with much longsuffering the vessels of wrath prepared for destruction, and that He might make known the riches of His glory on the vessels of mercy, which He had prepared beforehand for glory. (Rom 9:11–23)

What then? That which Israel is seeking for, it has not obtained, but *those who were chosen obtained it*, and the rest were hardened. (Rom 11:7)

For ye see your *calling*, brethren, how that not many wise men after the flesh, not many mighty, not many noble, are called: But God hath *chosen* the foolish things of the world to confound the wise; and God hath *chosen* the weak things of the world to confound the things which are mighty; and base things of the world, and things which are despised, hath God *chosen*, yea, and things which are not, to bring to nought things that are: That no flesh should glory in his presence. (1 Cor 1:26–29)

But we speak the wisdom of God in a mystery, even the hidden wisdom, which God *ordained before the world* unto our glory. (1 Cor 2:7)

For to you it *has been granted* for Christ's sake, *not only to believe* in Him, but also to suffer for His sake. (Phil 1:29)

It is *God who is at work in you, both to will* and to work for *His good pleasure*. (Phil 2:13)

Put on therefore, as the *elect* of God, holy and beloved, bowels of mercies, kindness, humbleness of mind, meekness, longsuffering. (Col 3:12)

Knowing, brethren beloved by God, His *choice* of you; for our gospel did not come to you in word only, but also in power and in the Holy Spirit and with full conviction; just as you know what kind of men we proved to be among you for your sake. (1 Thess 1:4–5)

That you would walk worthy of God, who has *called* you unto his kingdom and glory. (1 Thess 2:12)

For God has not destined us for wrath, but for obtaining salvation through our Lord Jesus Christ. (1 Thess 5:9)

But we are bound to give thanks to God always for you, brethren beloved by the Lord, because God from the beginning chose you for salvation through sanctification by the Spirit and belief in truth, to which He called you by our gospel, for the obtaining of the glory of our Lord Jesus Christ. (2 Thess 2:13, 14)

Who has saved us and called us with a holy calling, *not according to our works, but according to His own purpose and grace which was given to us in Christ Jesus before time began.* (2 Tim 1:9)

And all that dwell upon the earth shall worship him, whose names are *not written in the book of life* of the Lamb slain *from the foundation of the world*. (Rev 13:8)

The beast that you saw was, and is not, and will ascend out of the bottomless pit and go to perdition. And those who dwell on the earth will marvel, whose *names are not written in the Book of Life from the foundation of the world*, when they see the beast that was, and is not, and yet is. (Rev 17:8)

God's Predestinating Counsel

Your eyes have seen my unformed substance; / And in Your book they were all written, / The days that were ordained for me, / When as yet there was not one of them. (Psa 139:16)

Remember the former things long past, / For I am God, and there is no other; / I am God, and there is no one like Me, / Declaring the end from the beginning / And from ancient times things which have not been done, / Saying, "My purpose will be established, / And I will accomplish all My good pleasure." (Isa 46: 9–10)

For to do whatsoever Your hand and *Your counsel determined before* to be done. (Acts 4:28)

And when the Gentiles heard this, they were glad, and glorified the word of the Lord: and *as many as were ordained* to eternal life believed. (Acts 13:48)

We speak God's wisdom in a mystery, the hidden wisdom, which God *predestined before the ages* to our glory. (1 Cor 2:7)

Blessed be the God and Father of our Lord Jesus Christ, who has blessed us with every spiritual blessing in the heavenly places in Christ, just as He chose us in Him before the foundation of the world, that we should be holy and without blame before Him in love, having *predestined* us to adoption as sons by Jesus Christ to Himself, according to the good pleasure of His will, to the praise of the glory of His grace, by which He made us accepted in the Beloved. (Eph 1:3–5)

In Him also we have obtained an inheritance, *being predestined according to the purpose of Him who works all things according to the counsel of His will*. (Eph 1:12)

According to the *eternal purpose* which he purposed in Christ Jesus our Lord. (Eph 3:11)

For whom he did foreknow, he also did *predestinate* to be conformed to the image of his Son, that he might be the firstborn among many brethren. Moreover whom he did *predestinate*, them he also called: and whom he called, them he also justified: and whom he justified, them he also glorified. (Rom 8:29–30)

He has saved us, and called us with a holy calling, not according to our works, but according to His *own purpose* and grace which was *granted us in Christ Jesus from all eternity*. (2 Tim 1:9)

For there are certain men crept in unawares, who were *before of old ordained* to this condemnation, ungodly men, turning the grace of our God into lasciviousness, and deny–ing the only Lord God, and our Lord Jesus Christ. (Jude 4)

God's Choosing for Salvation

Then the King will say to those on His right, 'Come, you who are blessed of My Father, inherit the *kingdom prepared for you from the foundation of the world*.' (Matt 25:34)

Who shall lay any thing to the charge of God's *elect*? It is God that justifieth. (Rom 8:33)

For the children *being not yet born*, neither having done any good or evil, that the *purpose of God according to election* might stand, not of works, but of him that *calleth*. (Rom 9:11)

Even so then at this present time also there is a remnant according to the *election* of grace. . . . What then? Israel hath not obtained that which he seeketh for; but the *election* hath obtained it, and *the rest were blinded* (according as it is written, *God hath given them the spirit of slumber*, eyes that they should not see, and ears that they should not hear) unto this day. (Rom 11:5, 7–8)

Knowing, brethren beloved, your *election* of God. (1 Thess 1:4)

But we should always give thanks to God for you, brethren beloved by the Lord, because *God has chosen you from the beginning for salvation through sanctification by the Spirit and faith in the truth.* (2 Thess 2:13)

I charge thee before God, and the Lord Jesus Christ, and the *elect* angels, that thou observe these things without preferring one before another, doing nothing by partiality. (1 Tim 5:2)

Paul, a servant of God, and an apostle of Jesus Christ, according to the faith of God's *elect*, and the acknowledging of the truth which is after godliness; in hope of eternal life, which God, that cannot lie, *promised before the world began.* (Tit 1:1–2)

Elect according to the foreknowledge of God the Father, through sanctification of the Spirit, *unto obedience* and sprinkling of the blood of Jesus Christ: Grace unto you, and peace, be multiplied. (1 Pet 1:20)

The church that is at Babylon, *elected* together with you, saluteth you; and so doth Marcus my son. (1 Pet 5:13)

Wherefore the rather, brethren, give diligence to make your *calling* and *election* sure: for if ye do these things, ye shall never fall. (2 Pet 1:10)

Conclusion

Though I did not *expound* the teaching of these verses, I have at least shown that the notion of God's absolute sovereignty is abundantly displayed in Scripture. A theme appearing that frequently and in such a wide range of passages employing such an array of terms shows that it is not some side issue in the Bible. Perhaps opponents of predestination may spin a few verses as a means of countering the doctrine, but they will become quite dizzy if they attempt to spin such a great mass of evidence. Let us continue our study by more deeply engaging the subject of predestination.

Chapter 5
EXPLAINING ITS THEOLOGY

As we more directly engage predestination, we must once again recall that the *Westminster Confession* deems it a "high mystery" (WCF 3:8). We are finite creatures trying to comprehend the infinite God — and from a fallen, sin-polluted perspective at that. John Calvin warns that "he who does not expect more from God than he is able to comprehend in the scanty measure of his own reason, does him grievous wrong."[1]

Let us begin with the familiar word "providence." Most Christians believe in some form of divine providence in the world, for they do not hold that the world functions on its own apart from God. But the biblical doctrine of providence is a much more potent concept than generally held by non-predestinarian believers. Let us look at this as we move closer to a detailed explanation of predestination.

Defining Providence

Providence is the *historical* outworking of God's *pre-historical* plan by means of his *direct* superintendence. It focuses on God's overall, moment-by-moment governing of his creatures in accomplishing his eternal plan. Since providence is the outworking of God's eternal decree, his decree *precedes* providence and even *causes* it. God's providence is *active*, not reactive; that is, it *effects* historical

---

[1] Comments on Gen 18:13. Cited in Peter A. Lillback, *The Binding of God: Calvin's Role in the Development of Covenant Theology* (Grand Rapids: Baker, 2001), 204.

events rather than responds to them. Thus, the Confession has the following logical order in its chapters:

WCF 3: Of God's Eternal Decree
WCF 4: Of Creation
WCF 5: Of Providence

However, we are dealing with providence first, for rhetorical reasons. The general idea of God's providence is generally easier for Christians to recognize and accept. Just as we prepared ourselves for studying the doctrine of predestination by laying down some important issues to brace us for this jarring doctrine, here we are attempting to develop some "common ground" with non-predestinarian evangelicals. Nevertheless, I will be showing from Scripture that providence is really more strongly declared than the average Christian realizes. And this wedge issue will begin opening the door for understanding absolute predestination.

Historically theologians have defined "providence" in terms of three issues. Johannes Braunius (1628–1708) notes:

The acts of the providence of God are three: (1) He preserves all things in their being and duration; (2) He moves all things to their action by concurrence, in fact by precurrence; (3) He steers and guides all things to the desired end to which they were appointed from eternity.[2]

The second point may need further explication. It simply means that God controls all things by working in and through them ("concurrence"), not crushing and dominating them as if they were lifeless puppets. That is, his active influence occurs concurrently (simultaneously) with the historical action of the things themselves, it does not follow and respond to those actions. But his action is not merely *con*current, but even *pre*current, in that it is rooted in his

---

[2] Cited in Donald K. McKim, ed., *Encyclopedia of the Reformed Faith* (Louisville: Westminster, 1997), 306.

pre-existing plan. Point three simply means that God guides all historical actions to the final end that he appointed in eternity before creation.

The Confession defines providence in WCF 5:1 more clearly:

> God the great Creator of all things does uphold, direct, dispose, and govern all creatures, actions, and things, from the greatest even to the least, by His most wise and holy providence, according to His infallible foreknowledge, and the free and immutable counsel of His own will, to the praise of the glory of His wisdom, power, justice, goodness, and mercy.

The Shorter Catechism, which was produced along with the Confession, reads at SC Q. 11: "What are God's works of providence? A. God's works of providence are, his most holy, wise, and powerful preserving and governing all his creatures, and all their actions."

Detailing Providence

The doctrine of God's providence necessarily involves several key truths in filling it out. We will highlight these components of providence at this point, then later incorporate them into a fuller description of predestination itself. Let us consider four truths in this regard:

1. God has a plan
2. God's plan is eternal
3. God's plan is certain
4. God's plan is detailed

God has a plan
Scripture speaks of God's pre-temporal plan

We will note that God's plan for history is not some sort of "general idea" or "hopeful expectation for the big picture." Neither is it a stop-gap, responsive reaction to creaturely actions that God foresees falling out in history. Rather, his plan *effects* historical actions according to his predetermined purpose. His plan is expressly mentioned in a number of biblical passages, and is oftentimes called his "counsel" or "purpose."

One of the leading passages in this regard is Isaiah 46:10–11:

> Declaring the end from the beginning / And from ancient times things which have not been done, / Saying, 'My purpose will be established, / And I will accomplish all My good pleasure'; / Calling a bird of prey from the east, / The man of My purpose from a far country. / Truly I have spoken; truly I will bring it to pass. / I have planned it, surely I will do it.

Here we see that the "end" was declared already from "the beginning." God does not await the progress of history: he *causes* history's development and direction. And notice that he has a divine "purpose" that "will be established." He has planned and he will accomplish his purpose.

Another key passage is Acts 4:27–28:

> For truly in this city there were gathered together against Your holy servant Jesus, whom You anointed, both Herod and Pontius Pilate, along with the Gentiles and the peoples of Israel, to do whatever Your hand and Your purpose predestined to occur.

Note here that the "purpose" of God is "predestined" and it will "occur." And this predestined purpose involves individual men (Herod and Pilate) as well as groups of men ("the Gentiles" and "the peoples of Israel"). It is not general, with individuals accidentally wandering on stage as his drama unfolds.

The word "predestine" in Greek is: *prohorizo*. It is a compound of two words: *pro*, meaning "before" and *horizo*, from which we derive our word "horizon." Thus, it literally means "before the horizon." It means to establish an event before it even appears at a distance.

We will consider one final passage in this regard, Ephesians 3:11: "This was in accordance with the eternal purpose which He carried out in Christ Jesus our Lord." Here Paul expressly declares God's purpose as "eternal." It is his "eternal purpose": *prothesin ton aionon*, literally "plan of the eternity."

Predictive prophecy depends on God's pre-temporal plan

God's prophetic word announces portions of God's plan to us. We can trust the prophecies of Scripture because they are rooted in the sovereign plan of our eternal God, not simply because they reflect the good intention of a beneficent being.

> The Lord of hosts has sworn saying, "Surely, just as I have intended so it has happened, and just as I have planned so it will stand." (Isa 14:24)

> Declaring the end from the beginning and from ancient times things which have not been done, Saying, "My purpose will be established, And I will accomplish all My good pleasure; calling a bird of prey from the east, The man of My purpose from a far country. Truly I have spoken; truly I will bring it to pass. I have planned it, surely I will do it." (Isa 46:10–11)

> So shall My word be which goes forth from My mouth; / it shall not return to Me empty, / without accomplishing what I desire, / and without succeeding in the matter for which I sent it. (Isa 55:11)

> Therefore hear the plan of the Lord which He has planned against Edom, and His purposes which He has purposed against the inhabitants of Teman: surely they will drag them off, even the little ones of the flock; surely He will make their pasture desolate because of them. (Jer 49:20)

> The Lord has done what He purposed; / He has accomplished His word / Which He commanded from days of old. / He has thrown down without sparing, / And He has caused the enemy to rejoice

over you; / He has exalted the might of your adversaries. (Lam 2:17)

God's plan is eternal

His plan not only exists prior to the creation but is actually eternal, existing in God's mind forever. He did not create a world in which random forces control its ultimate outcome. He created a world on the basis of his eternal purpose.

> The counsel of the Lord *stands forever*, / The plans of His heart from generation to generation. (Psa 33:11)

> Then the King will say to those on His right, 'Come, you who are blessed of My Father, inherit the kingdom prepared for you *from the foundation of the world*.' (Matt 25:34)

> He chose us in Him *before the foundation of the world*, that we should be holy and blameless before Him. (Eph 1:4)

> This was in accordance with the *eternal purpose* which He carried out in Christ Jesus our Lord. (Eph 3:11)

> He has saved us, and called us with a holy calling, not according to our works, but according to *His own purpose* and grace which was granted us in Christ Jesus *from all eternity*. (2 Tim 1:9)

> His works were *finished* from the *foundation of the world*. (Heb 4:3b)

> In the same way God, desiring even more to show to the heirs of the promise the *unchangeableness of His purpose*, interposed with an oath. (Heb 6:17)

> Those who dwell on the earth will wonder, whose name has not been *written in the book of life from the foundation of the world*, when they see the beast, that he was and is not and will come. (Rev 17:8b)

God's plan is certain

God's plan is not merely his good intention or his holy desire that may or may not come to fruition, depending on man's willingness — or whatever other contingency we may consider. It is absolutely certain to transpire in history exactly as he determined it. In our human experience we often make plans that fail of their purpose; God does not. Though poet Robert Burns reminded us that "the best laid plans of mice and men often go astray," God's plans must not be equated with those "of mice and men."

God's eternal plan is absolutely sure because of who he is: He is the eternal Creator God and there is none like him in power, glory, and majesty. "His omnipotence is as sure a guarantee that the course of the world will conform to His plan as is His holiness a guarantee that all His works will be right."[3]

Therefore, Scripture presents his plan as *certain*:

God is not a man, that He should lie, Nor a son of man, that He should repent; Has He said, and will He not do it? Or has He spoken, and *will He not make it good*? (Num 23:19)

Many are the plans in a man's heart, / But *the counsel of the Lord, it will stand.* (Prov 19:21)

The Lord of hosts has sworn saying, 'Surely, *just as I have intended so it has happened*, and *just as I have planned so it will stand.*' (Isa 14:24)

Remember the former things long past, / For I *am God*, and there is no other; / I am God, and *there is no one like Me*, Declaring the end from the beginning / And from ancient times things which have not been done, / Saying, 'My purpose *will be established*, / And *I will accomplish* all My good pleasure'; / Calling a bird of prey from the east, /The man of My purpose from a far country. / Truly

---

[3] Loraine Boettner, *The Reformed Doctrine of Predestination* (Phillipsburg, N.J.: P & R, 1932), 31.

I have spoken; *truly I will bring it to pass.* / I have planned it, *surely I will do it.* (Isa 46:9–11)

For the vision is yet for the *appointed time*; / It hastens toward the goal, and *it will not fail.* / Though it tarries, wait for it; For *it will certainly come*, it will not delay. (Hab 2:3)

God's plan is detailed

God's eternal, certain plan is not a general scheme concerned with the "big things." After all, what things are "big" in the eyes of God?

Behold, the nations are like a drop from a bucket, / And are regarded as a speck of dust on the scales; / Behold, He lifts up the islands like fine dust. / Even Lebanon is not enough to burn, / Nor its beasts enough for a burnt offering. / All the nations are as nothing before Him, / They are regarded by Him as less than nothing and meaningless. / To whom then will you liken God? / Or what likeness will you compare with Him? (Isa 40:15–18)

Rather, God's plan determines *every detail of history* — all the way from the "big" events down to the most trivial matters, including the most mathematically precise atomic actions and the most apparently random events. He controls the farthest flung galaxy and the smallest atomic particle. His plan includes even the free choices of men and their wicked plans and actions.

1. God's plan includes cosmic issues

Thou alone art the Lord. Thou hast made the heavens, the heaven of heavens with all their host, the earth and all that is on it, the seas and all that is in them. Thou dost give life to all of them and the heavenly host bows down before Thee. (Neh 9:6)

And it is He who changes the times and the epochs; He removes kings and establishes kings; He gives wisdom to wise men, And knowledge to men of understanding. (Dan 2:21)

And all the inhabitants of the earth are accounted as nothing, / But He does according to His will in the host of heaven / And among the inhabitants of earth; / And no one can ward off His hand / Or say to Him, "What hast Thou done?" (Dan 4:35)

He is before all things, and in Him all things hold together. (Col 1:17)

And He is the radiance of His glory and the exact representation of His nature, and upholds all things by the word of His power. (Heb 1:3a)

2. God's plan includes even random events

He covers His hands with the lightning, and *commands it to strike the mark*. (Job 36:32)

The steps of a man are established by the Lord; / And He delights in his way. (Psa 37:23)

He sends forth springs in the valleys; / They flow between the mountains; / They give drink to every beast of the field; / The wild donkeys quench their thirst. . . . / He causes the grass to grow for the cattle, / And vegetation for the labor of man, / So that he may bring forth food from the earth, / And wine which makes man's heart glad, / So that he may make his face glisten with oil, / And food which sustains man's heart. . . . / The young lions roar after their prey, / And seek their food from God. (Psa 104:10-11, 14–15, 21)

He gives to the beast its food, / And to the young ravens which cry. . . . / He sends forth His command to the earth; / His word runs very swiftly. / He gives snow like wool; / He scatters the frost like ashes. / He casts forth His ice as fragments; / Who can stand before His cold? / He sends forth His word and melts them; / He causes His wind to blow and the waters to flow. (Psa 147:9, 15–18)

The mind of man plans his way, / But the Lord directs his steps. (Prov 16:9)

The king's heart is like channels of water in the hand of the Lord; / He turns it wherever He wishes. (Prov 21:1)

The lot is cast into the lap, / But its *every decision* is from the Lord. (Prov 16:33)

In whirlwind and storm is His way, / And clouds are the dust beneath His feet. (Nah 1:3b)

Are not two sparrows sold for a cent? And *yet not one of them will fall to the ground apart from your Father. But the very hairs of your head are all numbered.* (Matt 10:29–30)

3. God's plan includes destructive catastrophes

And as for Me, behold, I will harden the hearts of the Egyptians so that they will go in after them; and I will be honored through Pharaoh and all his army, through his chariots and his horsemen. (Exo 14:17; cp. Exo 4:21; 7:3; 9:12; 10:1, 20, 27; 11:10; 14:4, 8, 17)

But Sihon king of Heshbon was not willing for us to pass through his land; for the Lord your God hardened his spirit and made his heart obstinate, in order to deliver him into your hand, as he is today. (Deut 2:30)

For it was of the Lord to harden their hearts, to meet Israel in battle in order that he might utterly destroy them, that they might receive no mercy, but that he might destroy them, just as the Lord had commanded Moses. (Josh 11:20)

The Lord of hosts has sworn saying, "Surely, just as I have intended so it has happened, and just as I have planned so it will stand, to break Assyria in My land, and I will trample him on My mountains. Then his yoke will be removed from them, and his burden removed from their shoulder." This is the plan devised against the whole earth; and this is the hand that is stretched out against all the nations. For the Lord of hosts has planned, and who can frustrate it? And as for His stretched-out hand, who can turn it back? (Isa 14:24–27)

The One forming light and creating darkness, / Causing well-being and creating calamity; / I am the Lord who does all these. (Isa 45:7)

Who is there who speaks and it comes to pass, / Unless the Lord has commanded it? / Is it not from the mouth of the Most High / That *both good and ill* go forth? (Lam 3:37–38)

If a trumpet is blown in a city will not the people tremble? / If a calamity occurs in a city has not the Lord done it? (Amos 3:6)

4. *God's plan includes the evil actions of men*

Later we will study the moral questions arising from God's pre-determining all events, including evil acts. At that place I will demonstrate the truth of the Confessional statement:

God from all eternity, did, by the most wise and holy counsel of His own will, freely, and unchangeably ordain whatsoever comes to pass; yet so, as thereby neither is God the author of sin, nor is violence offered to the will of the creatures; nor is the liberty or contingency of second causes taken away, but rather established. (WCF 3:1)

Once again let us survey just a few samples of the clear, biblical declaration of this mysterious truth. I will make some brief comments regarding each of these:

Genesis 50:20

And as for you, *you meant evil* against me, but *God meant it for good* in order to bring about this present result, to preserve many people alive.

Here in Genesis 50:20 we read of Joseph's comments to his brother's who had sold him into slavery and lied to their father, claiming he had been killed (Gen 37:18–31). This evil action requires divine precurrence in that God "meant it for good." That is, God planned that Joseph would be moved from his home to Egypt in order to empower him so that he could spare Israel from famine. The evil-meaning brothers could *not* have killed Joseph; they could *not* have failed either to sell him or to sell him to the right caravan.

Because we currently "see through a glass darkly," we do not always see the ultimate purpose of God in such actions. Nevertheless, this is an historical sample that infallibly shows God does have a good design even in ordaining the evil acts of men. This is why we may confidently believe: "*He* works *all things* together for *good* to those who love the Lord who are called according to *his purpose*" (Rom 8:28).

Proverbs 16:14

The Lord has made everything for its own purpose, even the wicked for the day of evil.

This verse shows that God has in fact "made *everything* for *its own purpose*." This expressly includes even making "the wicked" for their end. (Later I will mention the doctrine of "reprobation," which speaks of the wicked's place in God's eternal plan regarding salvation.) The non-predestinarian would have to agree that God at least *knew* the wicked would ultimately be judged when he created them. So trying to "protect" God by declaring he did not predetermine evil in the world does not work: he creates wicked men even while perfectly knowing they will commit evil. Could not God have done otherwise? Why did he not create only people whom he foresaw would be saved? Or if free will demands that man have the prospect of great evil, why did he create him at all?

Luke 22:22

For indeed, the Son of Man is going as it has been *determined*; but *woe to that man* by whom He is betrayed!

Here Christ declares the absolutely, predetermined necessity of his betrayal. It could not have failed: it was *determined*. This word is from the Greek *horismenon*. It is the word that forms the base for the word "predestined" (*proorisen*). That which is "determined" is the evil betrayal of the Lord of glory (1 Cor 2:8; Jms 2:1), who had never sinned (2 Cor 5:21; 1 Pet 1:19), who had come to help men in their sinful estate (Heb 2:14–15; Gal 4:4). He was being betrayed (Matt 10:4; 26:25) by a covetous friend (Zech 13:6; Matt 26:50–51; John 12:4–6) and close associate (John 6:70–71), who knew he was innocent (Matt 27:3–4). He was being betrayed to a cruel, criminal death on the cross (Acts 2:23; Phil 2:8). This is surely the most sinful act in history.

Acts 2:23

This Man, delivered up by the *predetermined plan* and foreknow-ledge of God, you nailed to a cross by the hands of godless men and put Him to death.

Again we see the "predetermined plan" of God. This, of course, was revealed in prophecy long before it happened (Acts 3:18; 17:3; 26:23; cp. Luke 24:27). God's "foreknowledge" is rooted in his "predetermined plan," not vice versa. The "predetermined plan" translates the Greek phrase: *horismene* ("determined") *boule* ("plan"). Yet, he speaks to them as responsible men: "you nailed" / "you put to death." This involves the principle of precurrence I mentioned previously: God sovereignly ordains the act; man freely and respon-sibly commits it.

Acts 4:27–28

For truly in this city there were gathered together against Your
holy servant Jesus, whom You anointed, both Herod and Pontius
Pilate, along with the Gentiles and the peoples of Israel, *to do
whatever Your hand and Your purpose predestined to occur.*

Here we see a powerful declaration of the predestined plan of
God establishing the most evil act in history. The Greek phrase
reads: *he boule souprorisen genesthai.* The *boule* is God's "plan" (as in
Acts 2:23). The word *prohorizo* adds *pro* before *horizo* to express the
pre-historical nature of the divine determination. We must note
that it is intimately and personally determined by God's hand: *poi-
esai hosa he cheir sou* (literally: "to do whatever the hand of you").

We should note here that particular historical individuals are
included in the plan of God: Herod and Pontius Pilate, along with
the crowds of Jews and Gentiles. They were "gathered together" to
oppose "the holy servant Jesus" — in fact, they were "gathered
against" him. And their gathering against him historically effected
God's pre-temporal plan in bringing about the cruel death of Christ.

Conclusion

The familiar concept of providence is directly rooted in the fore-
boding concept of predestination. Virtually all Christians believe at
least in the basic idea of providence. Though, unfortunately, they
do not realize that providence entails God's absolute sovereignty
in predestination.

Now we are ready to touch on perhaps the most derided portion of predestination: God's sovereign determination to save some
but not all sinners. So now let us relate predestination to salvation.

Chapter 6
RELATING IT TO SALVATION

In the last chapter I demonstrated a *general* truth that is widely held among Protestant evangelicals: God governs history by his providence. All evangelicals believe that God is all-powerful, so that providential governance of the world is at least within God's capacity. After all, we believe God created all things, inspired the very words of Scripture, relates the future through prophecy, effects historical miracles, and answers prayers. Each of these actions demands that we recognize the reality of divine providence in time and on earth. Evangelicals are not deists: we believe that God is at work in governing the world.[1]

But I went further in showing from Scripture that God exercises his providence by means of a predetermined plan (a unilateral decision), a plan that is eternal (not responding to historical issues as they arise), certain (not a mere possibility), and detailed (not general). God does not providentially deal with history as a boxer ducking and weaving in order to gain the victory against a resistant opponent. *God's historical providence derives from his pre-historical plan.*

Now we must focus on the fundamental issue of the debate: predestination and election of certain men to eternal salvation. I have already surveyed a great number of verses to show that the Bible does speak of sovereignty, predestination, election, and so forth. I will now elaborate on several key passages specifically focusing on the question of God predestining individuals to their

---

[1] Deism may be defined most simply as: "belief in a God who created the world but has since remained indifferent to it" (Dictionary.com). Thus, the deist view of God holds that he only creates the world, he does not engage in it by direct supernatural revelation, active providential governance, or miracle.

eternal destinies. Following this, I will consider biblical, philosophical, and moral objections, finishing out our study of predestination.

General Biblical Evidence

As we consider a few key texts on election and predestination, we should note the remarkable fact that much of our understanding of the doctrine comes from Christ himself. Calvinists often point out that we trace our understanding from John Calvin (1509–64), back to Augustine (AD 354–430), through the Apostle Paul, and ultimately to Christ. This is pre-eminently a *biblical* doctrine rather than an ecclesiastical assertion by Presbyterians or Reformed Baptists.

Consequently, this doctrine will test your mettle as a Christian. I have surveyed many of the texts quickly. I will now focus and elaborate on predestination's leading texts. Once I finish this survey, we will see that the question of accepting the doctrine will boil down to four issues:

- Do I recognize the majesty of God? "For My thoughts are not your thoughts, / Neither are your ways My ways, declares the Lord. / For as the heavens are higher than the earth, / So are My ways higher than your ways, / And My thoughts than your thoughts" (Isa 55:8–9).

- Will I proclaim that God is true, regardless of my capacity to understand? "Let God be found true though every man a liar" (Rom 3:4)?

- Will I be sanctified as Christ prayed that his people would? "Sanctify them in the truth; Your word is truth" (John 17:17).

- Will I recognize the comfort of sovereign election? "My Father, who has given them to Me, is greater than all;

and no one is able to snatch them out of the Father's hand" (John 10:29).

Election and predestination are pre-temporal

The Scripture teaches that salvation occurs in history due to God's pre-historical, sovereign predestinating decree. If we locate salvation's root before the world began, then clearly it cannot be due to man's own action, which has not yet occurred. The pre-historical character of the decree absolutely forbids such a prospect.

Several clear passages underscore this fact and push us to predestinarian conclusions. I will highlight a few of the leading texts in this regard. But we should be aware that there are many more samples that could be brought to bear upon the subject.

1 Corinthians 2:7

We speak God's wisdom in a mystery, the hidden wisdom, which *God predestined before the ages* to our glory.

Notice how Paul associates "God's wisdom" with the concept of "mystery," calling it "the hidden wisdom" of God. Then he speaks of predestination from before history.

As I introduced the doctrine of predestination I noted that it will be a mystery to us, because of God's infinite wisdom and our fallen, finite knowledge. Though we may not be able to sort out the mystery of predestination, we must at least believe it as a feature of God's revelation in Scripture.

Ephesians 1:3–5

Blessed be the God and Father of our Lord Jesus Christ, who has blessed us with every spiritual blessing in the heavenly places in Christ, just as He *chose us* in *Him before the foundation of the world*, that we should be holy and blameless before Him. In love He *predestined* us to adoption as sons through Jesus Christ to Himself, according to the kind intention of His will.

This is *the* key passage on God's sovereignty in salvation. Here we have all the features of absolute predestination concentrated in one brief statement. The passage declares both that God "chose us" and that "he predestined us." It also locates *when* he chose and predestined us: "before the foundation of the world." It declares God's sovereignty to be an aspect of his "love" and an expression of his "kind intention," which are rooted in "his will."

How could the doctrine of predestination be stated more clearly? If we believe Paul's doctrine of salvation by grace through faith, which he discusses in Ephesians 2, we surely must believe his doctrine of predestination to salvation on the basis of God's will, which he discusses *in preparation for his free grace doctrine* in Ephesians 1. His predestination doctrine is the foundation for his free-grace doctrine. The two stand or fall together. Salvation is wholly by grace — and wholly determined by the pre-temporal plan of God.

Ephesians 1:11

In Him also we have obtained an inheritance, *being predestined according to the purpose of Him who works all things according to the counsel of His will.*

Here again in the same chapter Paul powerfully asserts predestination. He not only uses the critical term "predestine," but he secures predestination in "the purpose" of God and according to "the counsel of his will." Both "purpose" and "counsel" are strong words declaring God's sovereign plan. But he does even more: he makes predestination to salvation an aspect of God's larger program whereby he "works all things" in the universe.

2 Timothy 1:9

He has saved us and called us with a holy calling, *not according to our works, but according to His own purpose and grace which was given to us in Christ Jesus before time began.*

Ephesians 1 represents the leading passage on predestination, whereas this probably stands in third place just behind Romans 9. Paul clearly is speaking of salvation when he says "he has saved us." He sees salvation resulting from the "holy calling" of God: it is righteous and holy. And he makes sure that we not allow *any* aspect of salvation suggest our own effort, for he states that it is "not according to our works." Rather, salvation is 100% determined "according to his own purpose and grace."

God's sovereign purpose flows from his *undeserved* grace toward us. In fact, it is so disassociated from our effort that we receive it in Christ alone, and even "before time began."

Christianity differs from the other two leading monotheistic religions on this fundamental issue: Both Islam and Judaism involve systems of merit, whereas Christianity offers salvation purely on the basis of undeserved grace. In fact, this is a peculiar aspect of Christianity as a religious system which differs from *all* other religions — whether monotheistic or otherwise. And the doctrine of predestination is the foundation of that gracious work of God.

Election and predestination are absolutely sovereign

All of these five points that I am making are interrelated and will involve repetition even while providing expansion. I have just noted that predestination to salvation is determined in eternity before time began. This certainly speaks of its sovereignty. But now I will focus God's sovereignty a little more by means of the following verses. They are given in biblical order, rather than in order of significance.

Acts 13:48

When the Gentiles heard this, they began rejoicing and glorifying the word of the Lord; and as many *as had been appointed to eternal life* believed.

Here Luke is reporting on Paul's gospel preaching. He notes the Gentiles joyfully receiving the good news of salvation, even though the Jews reject it. He points out that "many" gentiles "believed." But he goes further and theologically explains *why* these Gentiles believed: they believed because they "had been appointed to eternal life." Indeed, he notes that *only* "as many as had been appointed to eternal life" actually responded in faith. Why did these respond, and not others? Because that is how many God had "appointed to eternal life."

The verb expression "had been ordained" is a passive, perfect participle. Its passive voice shows that it does not result from the believers themselves: They did not ordain; rather, they "had been ordained." Their salvation is the result of another's action, obviously God's. The expression is in the perfect tense, which speaks of a past action with a continuing result. They were ordained beforehand and their ordination continues to the present.

The verb "appointed" is not a word we have run into before. It is *tetagmenoi* from the verb *tasso*, which means "to inscribe or enroll." The idea here involves being enrolled in God's Book of Life, which is mentioned often in Scripture (Exo 32:32; Psa 69:28; Isa 4:3; Dan 12:1; Luke 10:20; Phil 4:3; Rev 3:5; 13:8; 17:8; 20:12; 21:27). The Book of Life contains the names of those who are to be saved.

Romans 8:29–30

For whom He foreknew, He also *predestined* to become conformed to the image of His Son, that He might be the first-born among many brethren; and whom He *predestined*, these He also called; and whom He called, these He also justified; and whom He justified, these He also glorified.

This famous passage presents "the golden chain of redemption." That is, it traces salvation from the beginning to the end, from before history began until after history concludes. It moves from God's foreknowing, to his predestining, calling, justifying, and glorifying us. Let us briefly consider each of these elements in the chain, especially since the first element is easily misunderstood.

We must begin with the word "foreknow." Some Christians believe that this word means "to foresee" or "to know something will happen in advance." They then assume that the second step in the chain of redemption, which is predestination, is determined by God because he looks down the corridors of time and foresees who would believe in him and respond to his gracious overtures. Then, on that foresight God chooses us and determines to secure our place in heaven. However, this is so mistaken that it actually turns the passage on its head and undermines all the other clear declarations of God's absolute sovereignty.

Notice what the passage actually says: "*whom* he foreknew." It does *not* say "*what* he foreknew." It does not say he foreknew something *about* someone (that the person would believe or call out for God's help). Rather, the verse declares that God foreknew the *person* himself. In other words, it does not state that God foreknew someone *would believe*. The person himself is the object of the verb "he foreknew."

Now we can detect the fundamental error in this Arminian understanding by demonstrating its absurdity.[2] Since the passage is speaking of those "whom he foreknew" we must consider the following. If it means those "whom God foresaw" are the ones who would be saved, we need to ask: Does not God foresee *everyone* who ever will exist? This interpretation of "foreknow" as "foresee" is caught on the horns of a dilemma: It either implies God does not foresee everyone in history (which undermines God's omniscience),

---

[2] This argumentative maneuver is called a *reductio ad absurdum* and is a helpful tool for demonstrating an erroneous argument. It effectively reduces the argument to an absurdity by showing its flawed implications. A *reductio* assumes a particular claim for the sake of argument, then draws out of that claim an absurd conclusion. By doing this, it demonstrates the original claim is erroneous because it allows for such an absurdity.

or it implies that he does in fact foresee everyone and that everyone will be saved (which denies Christian exclusivism). Thus, it either destroys God's knowledge or it leads to salvific universalism. Neither option is acceptable in an evangelical theology. And neither option is *possible* on a careful exegetical study of the passage.

Actually the word "foreknow" means "fore loved," or loved in advance. In Hebrew thought the word "know" often signifies "intimate knowledge, active delight, love." For instance, consider the use of "know" in the following passages:

> And Adam *knew* Eve his wife; and she conceived, and bare Cain, and said, I have gotten a man from the Lord. (Gen 4:1 KJV)

> For the Lord *knows* the way of the righteous, but the way of the wicked will perish. (Psa 1:6)

> You only have I *known* among all the families of the earth (Amos 3:2 KJV).

Furthermore, the concept of "foreknow" in this context cannot mean: "know in advance that someone will believe." That would lead to an absurdity in Romans 11:2: "God has not rejected His people whom He foreknew." Such an interpretation would have Paul declaring: "God has not rejected his people whom he foreknew would believe." Obviously that would not make sense; who could possibly think such? Why would God reject those whom he foreknew would believe? Rather this statement means: "God has not rejected his people whom he foreloved." Therefore, "foreknow" in Romans 8:29 obviously means "foreloved": "For whom he foreloved, them he also predestined."

Romans 9:15–16

> For He says to Moses, *I will have mercy on whom I have mercy*, and I will have compassion *on whom I have compassion*. So then it does

not depend on the man who wills or the man who runs, but on God who has mercy.

This is part of a passage that I believe is the second leading text on God's absolute sovereignty in predestination. It actually is even stronger than Ephesians 1 in that it is longer and deals with objections. However, it does not use the word "predestine," or I would have put it first. It is an extremely potent passage in declaring the absolute sovereignty of God's grace.

Here Paul cites Moses' record of God's statement: "*I will have mercy on whom I have mercy*, and I will have compassion *on whom I have compassion*." This shows that God's mercy is not our right to demand, but God's gift to give. In an age such as we live in, where everyone claims some right to this or that, predestination doctrine simply does not set well.

But once again we should remember that men are inherently rebellious sinners against their righteous Maker. Thus, they have no claim upon God. Mercy and compassion are God's to freely give to whomsoever he will. Once again we must remind ourselves that a major problem that non-Calvinists have in coming to terms with the doctrines of election and predestination is that they do not understand the enormity of sin. Without a proper understanding of sin, one cannot have an adequate understanding of grace.

Then Paul underscores this reality by declaring on his own authority as an apostle: "So then it does not depend on the man who wills or the man who runs, but on God who has mercy." I do not see anyway around this: Mercy is God's to give, not man's to claim. I will have more to say about this powerful Romans 9 passage in another context below.

Revelation 17:8

The beast that you saw was, and is not, and will ascend out of the bottomless pit and go to perdition. And those who dwell on the earth will marvel, whose *names are not written in the Book of*

Life from the foundation of the world, when they see the beast that was, and is not, and yet is.

The Book of Life imagery speaks of God's record of all those who will be saved. John teaches us that some are excluded from the Lamb's Book of Life — *from before the foundation of the world*. And if their name does not appear in the Book of Life, they will not be saved for: "if anyone's name was not found written in the Book of Life, he was thrown into the lake of fire" (Rev 20:15).

Election and predestination are totally unconditional

A number of verses underscore the unconditional nature of election and predestination. I will select only a few.

John 1:12–13

But as many as received Him, to them He gave the right to become children of God, even to those who believe in His name, *who were born* not of blood, nor of the will of the flesh, *nor of the will of man, but of God*.

We learn much about the new birth in John 3, with John 1 providing important supplementary information. All of this teaching supports the absolute sovereignty of God in salvation, as we shall see.

Here in John 1 Christ teaches that only one thing effects man's re-birth unto salvation: the will of God. Note that:

(1) The new birth is "not of blood." That is, the new birth is *not* based on man's bloodline. Literally the Greek speaks of "bloods" plural, which highlights a long genealogy (many forefathers), as in the case of a Jew with his long Old Testament lineage. Jews had a particular pride in their genealogy leading them to believe that being a descendent of Abraham was sufficient to merit God's favor. In Luke 3:8 Jesus rebukes the Jews who proudly claim "we have Abraham as our father" (see also John 8:31–59). Paul argues against

the Jewish racial pride noting that "there is neither Jew nor Greek" in Christ (Gal 3:28).

(2) The new birth is not by "the will of the flesh." That is, the new birth discounts sexual procreation ("the will of the flesh") as an element in salvation. For a man to determine to have children does not insure they will be saved. After all, "they are not all Israel who are descended from Israel; neither are they all children because they are Abraham's descendants, but: 'through Isaac your descendants will be named'" (Rom 9:6b–7).

(3) The new birth is not "of the will of man." That is, the new birth does not come by an act of man's will — however good he might strive to be. We must remember that Jesus taught that "no one *can* come to Me, unless the Father who sent Me draws him; and I will raise him up on the last day" (John 6:44). This is because we are "dead in trespasses and sins" (Eph 2:1). In Galatians 2:16 Paul writes: "knowing that a man is not justified by the works of the Law but through faith in Christ Jesus, even we have believed in Christ Jesus, that we may be justified by faith in Christ, and not by the works of the Law; since by the works of the Law shall no flesh be justified." Here we must recall that a proper understanding of predestination requires a proper view of sin, and man's inability.

(4) The new birth is not by any human action, "but of God." That is, the new birth is rooted solely in God's sovereign determinative action. This fits with all the other sovereignty verses we have studied thus far. It also prepares us for John 3 where Jesus focuses at length on the sovereignty of the new birth.

In John 3 Jesus engages the Pharisee Nicodemus in a discussion of the kingdom of God (salvation) and how man enters it. Jesus forthrightly declares that entry into God's kingdom is effected by something so totally outside of the individual's control that it is likened to the birth process itself: "Jesus answered and said to him, 'Truly, truly, I say to you, unless one is born again, he cannot see the kingdom of God'" (John 3:3). Who determines his own birth? The new birth must precede entry into the kingdom of God.

Furthermore, this spiritual new birth results from the Holy Spirit's action, not man's: "That which is born of the flesh is flesh, and that which is born of the Spirit is spirit" (John 3:6). This is why Paul even says that faith is "not of yourselves, it is a gift of God" (Eph 2:19). Man generates the birth of others in the fleshly world, but not the new birth in the spiritual realm.

Still further, that action of the Spirit is sovereign and unpredictable. It cannot be manipulated by man: "The wind blows where it wishes and you hear the sound of it, but do not know where it comes from and where it is going; so is everyone who is born of the Spirit" (John 3:8).

Thus, John's Gospel opens by declaring that no amount of genealogical pride, human reasoning, evangelistic manipulation, or stanzas of "Just As I Am" will save a person. Salvation comes unexpectedly, as the wind blows; it comes sovereignly, as God alone determines by his glorious wisdom. So then, not only does Scripture teach that "salvation is of the Lord" (Jon 2:9), but it also teaches that it is according to the Lord's timing.

2 Timothy 1:9

Who has saved us and called us with a holy calling, *not according to our works*, but according to His own purpose and grace which was given to us in Christ Jesus before time began.

I focused on this verse previously when I noted that salvation is rooted in the eternal realm before time began. Here I will highlight the phrase "not according to our works, but according to His own purpose." Salvation is absolutely unconditional. Note that this one verse powerfully drives home the concept of sovereign salvation. It provides several responses to any notion of human participation in effecting salvation, which also includes its being rooted in the fact that:

(1) God saves us: it is he "who has saved us." Salvation is solely of the Lord and is not a cooperative effort of God and man, since we are born "not of the will of the flesh, nor of the will of man, but of God" (John 1:13).

(2) God calls us: he "called us with a holy calling." When we respond to the gospel, it is because God is sovereignly "at work in you, both to will and to work for His good pleasure" (Phil 2:13).

(3) God disregards our works: salvation is "not according to our works." Salvation does not in any way depend upon our good works, since "those in the flesh cannot please God" (Rom 8:8).

(4) God effects his own purpose: we are saved "according to His own purpose." Salvation does not involve our good intentions, since "men loved the darkness rather than the light" (John 3:19).

(5) God saves by grace: we received the "grace which was granted us." His grace involves unmerited favor, since we do not deserve it because we are "dead in trespasses and sins" (Eph 2:1).

(6) God determines salvation before we exist: it derives "from all eternity." Salvation results from God's determination before we even exist in that "He chose us in Him before the foundation of the world" (Eph 1:4).

Election and predestination are specifically focused

God's predestinating action focuses on individuals, not solely on corporate masses such as the theocratic nation of Israel or the Church of Jesus Christ. God's saving mercies are particularistic, not generalistic.

> For just as the Father raises the dead and gives them life, even so the Son also gives life to *whom He wishes*. (John 5:21)

> All that the Father *gives Me* will come to Me, and the one who comes to Me I will by no means cast out. (John 6:37)

> *My sheep* hear My voice, and I know them, and they follow Me; and I give eternal life to them, and they shall never perish; and

no one shall snatch them out of My hand. My Father, who has *given them to Me*, is greater than all; and no one is able to snatch them out of the Father's hand. (John 10:27–29)

You did not choose Me, but I chose you and appointed you that you should go and bear fruit, and that your fruit should remain, that whatever you ask the Father in My name He may give you. (John 15:16)

Jesus spoke these words, lifted up His eyes to heaven, and said: "Father, the hour has come. Glorify Your Son, that Your Son also may glorify You, as You have given Him authority over all flesh, that *He should give eternal life to as many as You have given Him*." (John 17:1–2)

I ask on their behalf; I do not ask on behalf of the world, but *of those whom Thou hast given Me*; for *they are Thine*. (John 17:9)

Now when the Gentiles heard this, they were glad and glorified the word of the Lord. And *as many as had been appointed to eternal life believed*. (Acts 13:48)

The beast that you saw was and is not, and is about to come up out of the abyss and to go to destruction. And those who dwell on the earth will wonder, *whose name has not been written in the Book of Life from the foundation of the world*, when they see the beast, that he was and is not and will come. (Rev 17:8)

Specific Romans Evidence

Now we come to the most powerful passage in Scripture regarding God's sovereignty in salvation: Romans 9. Here Paul drives home the absolute sovereignty of God in various ways and by actually answering moral objections.

Though this passage can stand alone, we develop a greater appreciation for its instruction if we understand its contextual setting and argumentative purpose. Paul's great study of divine sovereignty does not just appear as an abstract observation. Rather, Paul is making a point regarding a particular theme in light of his readers' historical awareness. This passage is vitally connected with the flow and purpose of Romans, and we are always better off understanding verses in their contexts. And given the significance of this passage for our doctrine, I will quickly place it in its proper environment.

Some argue that this passage speaks only of Israel's national election and that it does not refer to predestinating individuals to salvation. Our study of the context will show the error of such an understanding. Still others point out that if God's election fails regarding the Jews as a nation, it is not an absolute determination among the Gentiles either. They would argue that all men are elect and that God has "voted for us" in that election. The final determination of the effectiveness of this election depends on whether we accept his election.

Consequently, a proper contextual understanding of this passage is necessary to show that it does not reduce election to a mere choice of corporate Israel. Nor does it teach that election is God's general good will toward all men.

The general flow of Romans

Paul establishes his theme early in Romans. At 1:16 he states: "I am not ashamed of the gospel, for it is the power of God for salvation to everyone who believes, to the Jew first and also to the Greek." Here we learn that the gospel is for all men, Jew and Gentile alike. This is an extremely important point in redemptive history, since God had focused on the Jews alone in the Old Testament:

> For you are a holy people to the Lord your God; the Lord your God has chosen you to be a people for His own possession out of all the peoples who are on the face of the earth. The Lord did not set His love on you nor choose you because you were more

in number than any of the peoples, for you were the fewest of all peoples (Deut 7:6–7)

See also Amos 3:2 and Psalm 147:19–20. Jesus even intentionally limited his ministry to Israel (Matt 10:5–6; 15:24).

But now the gospel is the very "power of God for salvation" *to all men*. This was a major issue in the New Testament, as we can see from Peter's experience regarding the Gentile Cornelius and his conversion in Acts 10; and Peter and Paul's involvement in the Jerusalem Council in Acts 15. Peter was initially rebuked for associating with the Gentile Cornelius (Acts 11:2–3), and the growing Church only reluctantly opened the door to the Gentiles in Acts 15:22–29 (cp. Acts 15:1–5).

Romans 1–8 develops the gospel, showing that all men are sinners in need of God's saving grace and that God is merciful to men of all races. For instance, Romans 1:18 shows that man is a sinner needing God's mercy: "The wrath of God is revealed from heaven against all ungodliness and unrighteousness of men, who suppress the truth in unrighteousness." This is true of Jew and Gentile alike in that "there is none righteous, not even one" (Rom 3:10).

Paul shows God's work with the Gentiles in Romans: "There will be tribulation and distress for every soul of man who does evil, of the Jew first and also of the Greek, but glory and honor and peace to every man who does good, to the Jew first and also to the Greek" (Rom 2:9–10). Thus, in the new covenant era "there is no distinction between Jew and Greek; for the same Lord is Lord of all, abounding in riches for all who call upon Him" (Rom 10:12).

Romans 8:28ff shows that God sovereignly saves sinners:

And we know that God causes all things to work together for good to those who love God, to those who are called according to His purpose. For whom He foreknew, He also predestined to become conformed to the image of His Son, that He might be the first-born among many brethren; and whom He predestined, these He also called; and whom He called, these He also justified; and whom He justified, these He also glorified. What then shall we say to these things? If God is for us, who is against us? He who did not spare His own Son, but delivered Him up for us all, how will He not also with Him freely give us all things? Who will bring a charge against God's elect? God is the one who justifies; who is the one who condemns? Christ Jesus is He who died, yes, rather who was raised, who is at the right hand of God, who also intercedes for us.

The specific setting of Romans 9

In Romans 9–11 Paul focuses on the question of the Jew for an important reason. If the gospel is the "power of God for salvation," the question naturally arises as to the situation with the Jews: What about the Jews then? Were they not God's chosen people, organized as the corporate nation of Israel? The "power of God" did not help them. Is God's saving work weak and ineffectual?

Paul answers with a resounding, "No, God's saving work is not ineffectual." He shows that despite the failure of the majority of the Jews to follow Christ, the gospel remains the "power of God." And now in Romans 9–11 he explains the problem of the Jew in defending God's powerful gospel.

This is important for his overall message, since he argues that Abraham the father of the Jews is also the father of all believers, Jew and Gentile alike. "Abraham received the sign of circumcision, a seal of the righteousness of the faith which he had while uncircumcised, that he might be the father of *all who believe* without being circumcised, that righteousness might be reckoned to them" (Rom 4:11). "For the promise to Abraham or to his descendants that he would be heir of the *world* was not through the Law, but through the righteousness of faith" (Rom 4:13). The problem Paul is dealing with is crucial: If any supposes that the powerful gospel fails for the

Jews, perhaps it could fail for us as well. Paul must address this problem.

So in Romans 9–11 Paul defends the gospel as the "power of God for salvation" for all men by explaining the problem of Jewish unbelief in the light of God's sovereignty. Remember, just a few verses before Romans 9, he emphasizes God's sovereignty in individual salvation (Rom 8:28–39). So then, the theological claim of God's sovereignty seems to clash head-on with the historical problem of the Jews. Why did they fail to gain salvation since Israel was the elect nation? How can Paul answer the problem arising from their failure?

He answers this perplexity by developing the doctrine of God's sovereignty more fully than anywhere else in Scripture. Despite the Jewish apostasy that all can see, God's word has *not* failed; the gospel *is* the power of God for salvation! Let us note how he shows this.

After he deals with the matter of the Jews in the light of God's powerful gospel and by affirming God's absolute sovereignty among men, he ends the first section of Romans (chs. 1–11) with a glorious and resounding praise to God's almighty power:

> Oh, the depth of the riches both of the wisdom and knowledge of God! How unsearchable are His judgments and unfathomable His ways! For who has known the mind of the Lord, or who became His counselor? Or who has first given to Him that it might be paid back to him again? For from Him and through Him and to Him are all things. To Him be the glory forever. Amen. (Rom 11:33–36)

Truly God's wisdom, knowledge, and judgment are unfathomable. We cannot presume to plumb the depths of his infinite, eternal mind. After all, "all things" of the universe are from him (he determined to create all things), through him (he actually created all things by his word), and to him (all things exist for his glory and his alone). We can only bow in awe and adoration with hearts filled with praise at the being, power, and majesty of our God.

Paul explains the problem of Jewish salvation in the light of his theme of gospel power:

> But it is not as though the word of God has failed. For they are not all Israel who are descended from Israel; neither are they all children because they are Abraham's descendants, but: "through Isaac your descendants will be named." That is, it is not the children of the flesh who are children of God, but the children of the promise are regarded as descendants. For this is a word of promise: "At this time I will come, and Sarah shall have a son" (Rom 9:6–9).

He expressly denies the prospect of God's work having "failed." Actually the "failure" of God's sovereignty regarding the Jews is only apparent, not real. In fact, the very reason for the apparent failure of God's word is *because of* the reality of the God's sovereign promise.

God's word sovereignly differentiates men in history. Paul provides two historical illustrations of this.

First, he teaches us in no uncertain terms that not all Israel is "truly" Israel. Though Abraham is chosen by God to be the father of believers, God's divine call comes through his son by Sarah (i.e., Isaac), not through his son by his handmaiden Hagar (i.e., Ishmael). Sarah's seed was the seed of promise to Abraham, whereas Hagar's was Abraham's attempt at helping God achieve the promise ("the will of the flesh," John 1:13).

Second, he further elucidates God's sovereignty by pointing to Rebecca's seed. He once again sorts out the promise in history, as he moves from Sarah's seed to Rebekah's. Now he points out that even twins in the same womb are subject to God's sovereignty, and that the issue is not which *corporate* seed line God prefers, i.e., Sarah's entire seed line over against Hagar's. In fact, God confounds

human expectations by choosing the second born over the first
born even in Rebekah's seed line:

> And not only this, but there was Rebekah also, when she had
> conceived twins by one man, our father Isaac; for though the
> twins were not yet born, and had not done anything good or bad,
> in order that God's purpose according to His choice might stand,
> not because of works, but because of Him who calls, it was said
> to her, "The older will serve the younger." Just as it is written,
> "Jacob I loved, but Esau I hated." (Rom 9:10–13)

It is at this point that Paul launches out into a full, vigorous
discussion of God's powerful sovereignty. He shows that even
though salvation is to the Jew first, God nevertheless differentiates
between persons even among the Jews. Paul is therefore arguing
here that there is a *remnant*; Israel's failure is not total. God's power
preserves a portion of Israel. In Romans 11 he will show Israel's
failure is not *permanent*: God will call the mass of Israel back to
himself in the future. In both matters, God stands sovereign over
the affairs of men.

The basic argument in Romans 9

Now we are ready to actually start unpacking Romans 9 to show
how vigorously Paul asserts the doctrine of absolute predestination.

God sovereignly chooses the second born child over the first
born child, even before they were born:

> for though the twins were not yet born, and had not done
> anything good or bad, in order that God's purpose according to
> His choice might stand, not because of works, but because of
> Him who calls, it was said to her, "The older will serve the young-
> er." (Rom 9: 11–12)

Clearly their merit or demerit had nothing to do with God's motive
to election. This is true whether by intrinsic merit that might be
assumed (since they were the seed of the covenant) or due to any

foreseen acts of faithfulness or righteousness after they were born. The text clearly states Jacob was chosen before either he or his twin were born and before either had done any "good or bad." God did not choose Jacob, nor reject Esau due to their own status or efforts.

Then Paul further grounds this choice in God's absolute sovereignty. He notes that God's choice was so that "the purpose of God according to election might stand, not of works, but of him who calls." God's election "stands." Man's works are discounted. God calls, man does not seek.

Again, the election here is not simply regarding corporate Israel, the theocratic election of Israel as a nation, as some argue. Paul is not declaring that the nation as such was elect, so that election does not apply to individuals but to only that peculiar nation as a body. Note evidences against such an interpretation:

First, the individual focus. Paul mentions specific historical individuals in his discussion of election: Jacob and Esau. It is true that in its original setting in Malachi 1, the prophet was explaining God's judgment on two nations, the people of Israel and the people of Edom who flow from Jacob and Esau. But whatever we might think of the question of the two nations flowing from these two individuals, the fact is that Paul specifically mentions two individuals. He declares "Jacob have I loved, Esau have I hated." These are individual twins from the same womb. In fact, though they both were progenitors of different nations, Paul traces the different status accorded to each nation to God's differentiating love, which separates Jacob personally from Esau. Paul is focusing on the individual as such.

Second, the particular objection. Paul is answering the objection: How can we claim God has absolutely sovereign power if the mass of Israel is lost — that is, if most of the individuals from the corporate nation are in rebellion? Thus, his concern is not with national election irrespective of individuals in the nation, because he is concerned with the fact that most of the individual members of Israel are in rebellion. Individuals make the difference. The election he is dealing with is personal, individual election to salvation.

Third, the specific observation. Paul clearly asserts: "they are not all Israel, who are of Israel" (Rom 9:6b). That is, the fact that Israel is an elect nation does not prove that all the individual members of that nation are elected for salvation. Many individuals in the nation are not part of the gracious election to salvation; but many individuals are. That is, they are not all elect individuals who are members of the elect nation. The question is: Why are so many individuals in rebellion and so few faithful? His answer is: Because of God's discriminating love exercised in choosing individuals from the mass of Israel.

Fourth, the additional concurrence. In Romans 11:5, 7 Paul uses the term "election" again when he speaks of "a remnant according to the election of grace." This speaks of a small number of individuals who are truly elect by grace from within the nationally elect nation. If "election" speaks only of national election, how can he speak of a "remnant according to election"? That would not make sense. We must distinguish national, theocratic election from personal, salvific election to understand Paul's point here.

Fifth, the association of terms. Paul associates the concepts of "call" and "works" together in Romans 9:10: "not because of works, but because of him who calls." Paul regularly employs these words in the discussions of personal salvation. He speaks of the "call" to salvation in 1 Corinthians 1:9; 7:15; Galatians 1:6, 15; 5:8, 13; Ephesians 4:1, 4; Colossians 3:15; 1 Thessalonians 2:12; 4:7; 5:24; 2 Thessalonians 2:14; 1 Timothy 6:12; and 2 Timothy 1:9.

In fact, he speaks of God's sovereignly calling individuals to salvation in the very context under scrutiny: "Whom He predestined, these He also called; and whom He called, these He also justified; and whom He justified, these He also glorified" (Rom 8:30) and "even us, whom He also called, not from among Jews only, but also from among Gentiles" (Rom 9:24).

Sixth, the human response. When Paul considers the human response to such information, he clearly focuses on the question of individual election to salvation, rather than national destinies. We will focus on this passage below, but here we simply note it: "What shall we say then? There is no injustice with God, is there? May it never be! For He says to Moses, 'I will have mercy on whom I have mercy, and I will have compassion on whom I have compassion.' So then it does not depend on *the man* who wills or *the man* who runs, but on God who has mercy" (Rom 9:14–16).

So then, the election Paul is focusing on in Romans 9 is not corporate election to status as a nation, but individual election to salvation — even from among the members of that nation. It shows that God's saving election discriminates and differentiates between *individuals*. Truly, God elects us before we are born and according to his purpose irrespective of our works, according to Romans 9:10.

The moral objection in Romans 9

Now we should note that Paul considers the human indignation against such a prospect:

> What shall we say then? There is no injustice with God, is there? May it never be! For He says to Moses, "I will have mercy on whom I have mercy, and I will have compassion on whom I have compassion." (Rom 9:14–15)

Paul vigorously responds to the objection that God would be unjust if he chose one over another for salvation: "May it never be!" Here the Greek phrase is *me genoito*, the strongest form of negation in Greek.

In verse 15 Paul quotes Exodus 33:19: "I will have mercy on whom I have mercy." This does not seem to answer the objection as to whether God is unjust. But we must be aware of two issues:

(1) Paul's point is: This is not simply me saying this, this is a part of the Scriptures that you all know to be true. (2) God's choosing is not a matter of justice, but of mercy. All men deserve wrath on the grounds of justice. Paul emphasizes the unconditional determination of God in granting *mercy*: "So then it does not depend on the man who wills or the man who runs, but on God who has mercy" (Rom 9:16). This is his conclusion to the argument, hence he says: "So then." That is, if it is true that God has mercy on whom he wills to have mercy, two negative conclusions follow:

1. Man's will is not determinative; God's is: "it does not depend on the man who wills."

2. Man's self exertion is not determinative: "it does not depend on . . . the man who runs."

Salvation does not result from attainment by man, but by mercy from God. This fits with everything we have learned in Scripture about the absoluteness of God's sovereignty. Neither man's desires nor his determination secure God's favor. It is freely given by God to undeserving sinners of his own choosing.

> For the Scripture says to Pharaoh, "For this very purpose I raised you up, to demonstrate My power in you, and that My name might be proclaimed throughout the whole earth." So then He has mercy on whom He desires, and He hardens whom He desires. (Rom 9:17–18)

Here Paul brings forward another confirmation from Scripture, this time declaring the opposite of mercy in God's ways with men. Not all men are recipients of his mercy. God's sovereignty is not abstract, but concrete: it deals with real men in actual history: God raises up the individual Pharaoh and *hardens* him.

Though Scripture does speak of Pharaoh hardening his own heart (Exo 7:13; 8:32; 9:34), it more often mentions the prior hardening by God (Exo 4:21; 7:3; 9:12; 10:1, 20, 27; 11:10; 14:4, 8).

We must remember that all men are already guilty before God and fallen in his sight. Thus, God is not hardening an innocent, helpless individual who might have chosen better. God's sovereignty is ultimate both in salvation and in destruction for Paul parallels the two, opposite actions of God.

Paul considers the objection that this is unfair because no man can resist God's power:

> You will say to me then, "Why does He still find fault? For who resists His will?" On the contrary, who are you, O man, who answers back to God? The thing molded will not say to the molder, "Why did you make me like this," will it? Or does not the potter have a right over the clay, to make from the same lump one vessel for honorable use, and another for common use? What if God, although willing to demonstrate His wrath and to make His power known, endured with much patience vessels of wrath prepared for destruction? And He did so in order that He might make known the riches of His glory upon vessels of mercy, which He prepared beforehand for glory. (Rom 9:19–23).

This objection flows from what precedes in verse 18: If God hardens whom he wills, how can a man resist the will of God? Man is helpless before Almighty God. How, then, can we find fault with such a helpless person? Paul strengthens the objection by adding the complaint: "For who resists His will?"

This is a common complaint against absolute predestination. The objection is made universal by asking rhetorically: "Who resists His will?" This asks if there is anyone in all of creation who has, in fact, resisted his will. We must feel the strength of the objection if we are to sense the power in Paul's affirming God's sovereignty. Since no one has ever resisted God's will, how can God hold *anyone* responsible for their actions? Men appear to be crushed under the wheel of providence, mere puppets on the stage of history dangling under the irresistible hand of God.

Paul's answer is basically that Christians must stand in humble, reverential silence before the majesty of God: "On the contrary, who are you, O man, who answers back to God?" Bluntly put, the answer is: "Who are *you*?" (Rom 9:20a). Notice the important contrast in Paul's statement between "O man" and "God." Here we have the fallen, finite, temporal creature called to silence before the holy, infinite, eternal Creator. Or as Paul metaphorically puts it: We must consider the mere lump of clay in the hand of the Almighty Potter (Rom 9:21). This is vitally important for us to recognize in our approaching God. In effect, Paul is confronting the objector with the following line of reasoning: "Think of who God is! Now realize who you are! What in the world are you up to?"

Already in Romans 1 Paul was establishing the Creator/creature distinction: "For they exchanged the truth of God for a lie, and worshiped and served the creature rather than the Creator, who is blessed forever. Amen" (Rom 1:25). This, of course, furthers the theme of the book stated in Romans 1:16: "For I am not ashamed of the gospel, for it is the power of God for salvation to everyone who believes, to the Jew first and also to the Greek."

Remember that Paul ends this section on God's sovereignty and the problem of Israel's disbelief (which covers Rom 9–11) by declaring: "Oh, the depth of the riches both of the wisdom and knowledge of God! How unsearchable are His judgments and unfathomable His ways! For who has known the mind of the Lord, or who became His counselor? . . . For from Him and through Him and to Him are all things. To Him be the glory forever. Amen." (Rom 11:33, 34, 36)

In effect, Paul directs us to take Job's course of action when he complained against God:

> Then the Lord said to Job, / "Will the faultfinder contend with the Almighty? / Let him who reproves God answer it." / Then Job answered the Lord and said, / "Behold, I am insignificant; what can I reply to Thee? / I lay my hand on my mouth. / Once I have

spoken, and I will not answer; / Even twice, and I will add no more." (Job 40:1–5)

Then Job answered the Lord, and said, / "I know that Thou canst do all things, / And that no purpose of Thine can be thwarted. / Who is this that hides counsel without knowledge? / Therefore I have declared that which I did not understand, / Things too wonderful for me, which I did not know. / Hear, now, and I will speak; / I will ask Thee, and do Thou instruct me. / I have heard of Thee by the hearing of the ear; / But now my eye sees Thee; / therefore I retract, / And I repent in dust and ashes." (Job 42:1–6)

In truth I know that this is so, / But how can a man be in the right before God? / If one wished to dispute with Him, / He could not answer Him once in a thousand times. / Wise in heart and mighty in strength, / Who has defied Him without harm? / It is God who removes the mountains, they know not how, / When He overturns them in His anger. . . . / Who does great things, unfathomable, / And wondrous works without number. . . . / How then can I answer Him, / And choose my words before Him? (Job 9:2–5, 10, 14)

Behold, let me tell you, you are not right in this, / For God is greater than man. / Why do you complain against Him, / That He does not give an account of all His doings? (Job 33:12–13)

Let us note Paul's assumption, his methodology, and the implication of his answer. These are quite important for us to recognize as God's humble servants.

Paul's assumption: Our God is absolute; we are comparatively nothing. The whole passage breathes the atmosphere of God's sovereignty to do as he pleases. This core assumption provides the foundational principle by which he responds to the objection against God's sovereignty.

Paul's methodology: Because of his assumption we must operate in humility before God. God does not have to answer our objections. We are but men; he is the Almighty God.

Paul's implication in his answer: Paul does not correct the questioner by stating that his objection is based on a faulty understanding of his teaching. He does not say: "You are mistaken in your understanding of what I am saying." He accepts the premise of the objection, then rebukes the objector for arrogance, not for ignorance. In fact, Paul continues on in such a way as to further establish the absoluteness of God's will, by using the imagery of a potter working on clay:

> On the contrary, who are you, O man, who answers back to God? The thing molded will not say to the molder, "Why did you make me like this," will it? Or does not the potter have a right over the clay, to make from the same lump one vessel for honorable use, and another for common use? What if God, although willing to demonstrate His wrath and to make His power known, endured with much patience vessels of wrath prepared for destruction? And He did so in order that He might make known the riches of His glory upon vessels of mercy, which He prepared beforehand for glory. (Rom 9:20–23)

John Calvin writes of this verse: "Why, then, did [Paul] not make use of this short answer, but assign the highest place to the will of God, so that it alone should be sufficient for us, rather than any other cause? If the objection that God reprobates or elects according to His will those whom He does not honor with His favor, or towards whom He shows unmerited love — if this objection had been false, Paul would not have omitted to refute it."

The overall point of Romans 9

The lessons on God's absolute sovereignty in election are countless, clear, and compelling. Just consider the following litany of observations.

1. God sovereignly separates some Jews out of his chosen nation: "they are not all Israel who are of Israel . . . the

children of the promise are regarded as descendants" (Rom 9:7–9).

2. God's sovereign election precedes our birth in history: "for though the children were not yet born" (Rom 9:10a).

3. God's sovereign election is not a response to any foreseen good or faithfulness in the object of election: he chooses some and rejects others even though they "had not done anything good or bad" (Rom 9:10b).

4. God's sovereign election is according to his own determination: "in order that God's purpose according to his choice might stand, not because of works but because of him who calls" (Rom 10:9c).

5. God's sovereign election is underscored by God's own claim: "I will have mercy upon whom I will have mercy" (Rom 10:15).

6. God's sovereign election is emphasized by discounting optional possibilities to explain the flow of God's mercy: "So then it does not depend on the man who wills or the man who runs, but on God who has mercy" (Rom 9:16).

7. God's sovereign election is seen in historic examples: "For the Scripture says to Pharaoh, For this very purpose I raised you up, to demonstrate My power in you, and that My name might be proclaimed throughout the whole earth'" (Rom 9:17).

8. God's sovereign election appears in both his mercy and wrath: "So then He has mercy on whom He desires, and He hardens whom He desires" (Rom 9:18).

9. God's sovereign election cannot be discounted by man: "On the contrary, who are you, O man, who answers back to God?" (Rom 9:20a).

10 God's sovereign election can be symbolized by the authority of the potter over the clay: "The thing molded will not say to the molder, 'Why did you make me like this,' will it? Or does not the potter have a right over the clay, to make from the same lump one vessel for honorable use, and another for common use?" (Rom 9:20b–21).

11 God's sovereign election is designed to bring glory to God alone: "He did so in order that He might make known the riches of His glory upon vessels of mercy, which He prepared beforehand for glory" (Rom 9:23).

Paul closes the mouth of the objector. God is an absolute sovereign, who does as he pleases and according to his own character.

Chapter 7
RESOLVING THE DIFFICULTIES

We have taken the time not only to define predestination (Ch. 2) but to properly understand the parties involved in it (Ch. 3). Then we spent two chapters presenting and defending predestination and the absolute sovereignty of God from Scripture (ch. 4) and theology (ch. 5). We then applied the doctrine to salvation (ch. 6). Now we must confront the difficulties arising from this perplexing doctrine.

As Christians we are committed to the voice of God speaking in Scripture. In fact, as conservative, evangelical Christians we hold to the plenary, verbal inspiration and authority of the Word of God. "Plenary" inspiration means that *all* Scripture is inspired; "verbal" inspiration means *every word* is inspired.

> The words of the Lord are pure words; / As silver tried in a furnace on the earth, refined seven times. (Psa 12:6:)

> Every word of God is tested. (Prov 30:5a)

> All scripture is given by inspiration of God, and is profitable for doctrine, for reproof, for correction, for instruction in righteousness: That the man of God may be perfect, throughly furnished unto all good works. (2 Tim 3:16–17)

> Knowing this first, that no prophecy of the scripture is of any private interpretation. For the prophecy came not in old time by the will of man: but holy men of God spake as they were moved by the Holy Ghost. (2 Pet 1:20–21)

Therefore, our fundamental method for resolving the question regarding predestination involved a study of God's Word (see ch. 4). God determines doctrinal truth, not our traditional convictions, intellectual capacity, emotional sympathies, or moral expectations. But all too often the latter issues control the Christian's thinking on the subject. Nevertheless, with Isaiah we must declare: "to the law and to the testimony: if they speak not according to this word, it is because there is no light in them" (Isa 8:20). After all Jesus prayed for us accordingly: "Your word is truth, sanctify them through Your truth" (John 17:17). Thus, as Paul expresses it, we must: "let God be found true, though every man be found a liar" (Rom 3:4).

We must answer two questions that potentially plague our analysis of predestination. These questions not only can strengthen us when dealing with predestination doctrine, but alert us to the inherent danger in resisting it. Those two questions are:

- Is predestination a unique problem?

- May I question God?

Is Predestination a Unique Problem?

Predestination is heralded as one of the most difficult doctrines in Scripture. Our minds boggle at trying *intellectually* to comprehend and *morally* to justify the absolute sovereignty of God which comes to expression in predestination and involves our free will.

- *Logically* how can we comprehend these two seemingly contradictory doctrines, predestination and free will? If God predetermines our actions, how can we be free? This seems logically absurd and contrary to our rational understanding.

- *Morally* how can we accept predestination with all that it entails? How could a perfect, just God irrevocably predetermine the eternal destinies of men created in his image? If God determines our actions, how can we be responsible? Predestination seems unfair and immoral, and as such is repugnant to our moral sensibilities.

These are large issues. However, we must be careful about adopting a method that causes us to balk at doctrines that confound and repel us. Why? Because the Bible is our ultimate method for understanding God, and it records a great number of "difficult" and "repugnant" doctrines. Shall we deny them all?

Let us consider just a few well-known and widely-accepted difficult and "repugnant" doctrines of Scripture. Once we see how some of our most basic, well-received doctrines also suffer from moral repugnance and intellectual difficulty, we will be more open to accepting the doctrine of predestination. Or at least we will have to drop such challenges to the doctrine.

Intellectually difficult doctrines

The Trinity

Wayne Grudem defines the Trinity in this way: "God eternally exists as three persons, Father, Son, and Holy Spirit and each person is fully God, and there is one God."[1] The Confession expresses the doctrine thus:

> WCF 2:3: "In the unity of the Godhead there be three persons, of one substance, power, and eternity: God the Father, God the Son, and God the Holy Ghost: the Father is of none, neither begotten, nor proceeding; the Son is eternally begotten of the Father; the Holy Ghost eternally proceeding from the Father and the Son."

> WCF 8:2: "The Son of God, the second person of the Trinity, being very and eternal God, of one substance and equal with the Father."

The Trinity is a doctrine unique among all world religions. It is a doctrine that virtually defines true Christianity. Yet it is a doctrine fraught with intellectual challenges — in that we hold there is only

---

[1] Wayne Grudem, *Systematic Theology: An Introduction to Biblical Doctrine* (Grand Rapids: Zondervan, 1994), 226.

one God, while simultaneously holding that the Father, the Son, and the Holy Spirit are each God. As a result of this doctrine, evangelical theologians confess a problem.

Thomas C. Oden declares: "The idea that the one God meets us in three persons is thought to be among the most opaque and least accessible of all Christian teachings."[2] Millard Erickson states:

> "Christianity is the only major religion that makes this claim about God. Numerous attempts have been made to understand this profound truth. Some have led to distortions of this very important doctrine."[3] He continues: "In the doctrine of the Trinity, we encounter one of the truly distinctive doctrines of Christianity. Among the religions of the world, the Christian faith is unique in making the claim that God is one and yet there are three who are God. Although it seems on the surface to be a self-contradictory doctrine . . . nevertheless, devout minds have been led to it as they sought to do justice to the witness of Scripture."[4]

Thus, the most fundamental and distinctive doctrine of the Christian faith involves intellectually incomprehensible features. Yet evangelical, orthodox Christians still affirm the doctrine of the Trinity. To accept a method (a refusal to accept intellectual incomprehensibility) that leads us to reject difficult doctrines (such as predestination) opens the prospect of either rejecting other fundamental doctrines or exposing us to enduring charges of inconsistency in accepting some difficult doctrines while rejecting others.

---

[2] Thomas C. Oden, *The Living God: Systematic Theology*, vol. 1 (Peabody, Mass.: Prince, 1987), 181.

[3] Millard J. Erickson, *Christian Theology* (Grand Rapids: Baker, 1998), 346.

[4] Erickson, *Christian Theology*, 347.

The two natures of Christ

Wayne Grudem defines the biblical doctrine of Christ's person: "Jesus Christ was fully God and fully man in one person, and will be so forever."[5] The Confession expresses this doctrine similarly:

> The Son of God, the second person of the Trinity, being very and eternal God, of one substance and equal with the Father, did, when the fullness of time was come, take upon Him man's nature, with all the essential properties, and common infirmities thereof, yet without sin; being conceived by the power of the Holy Ghost, in the womb of the virgin Mary, of her substance. So that two whole, perfect, and distinct natures, the Godhead and the manhood, were inseparably joined together in one person, without conversion, composition, or confusion. Which person is very God, and very man, yet one Christ, the only Mediator between God and man. (WCF 8:2)

The doctrine of the two-natured Christ has long been assaulted as unintelligible. According to Wayne Grudem, John Hick argues in *The Myth of God Incarnate* (1977) that this doctrine "has never been a coherent or intelligible doctrine through the history of the church."[6] Grudem responds:

> The assertion that "Jesus was fully God and fully man in one person," though not a contradiction, is a paradox that we cannot fully understand in this age and perhaps not for all eternity, but this does not give us the right to label it "incoherent" or "unintelligible". . . . Our proper response [to unbelieving challenges] is not to reject the clear and central teaching of Scripture about the incarnation, but simply to recognize that it will remain a paradox, that this is all that God has chosen to reveal to us about it, and that it is true.[7]

---

[5] Grudem, *Systematic Theology*, 529.
[6] Grudem, *Systematic Theology*, 552.
[7] Grudem, *Systematic Theology*, 553.

Millard Erickson expresses the objections to the two-natured Christ: "The problems of Christology were posed largely in terms of metaphysics: How can the divine nature and the human nature coexist within one person? Or, to put it differently, how can Jesus be both God and man at once?" He notes that philosophers argue against understanding Christ as possessing two natures: "It is neither necessary nor possible to do so." He then confesses as an orthodox Christian: "To be sure, there is a paradox here, a concept that is very difficult to assimilate intellectually."[8]

The union of the divine and human natures in one person is called the "hypostatic union"[9] by theologians. And even though we cannot fully comprehend how Christ is 100% God and 100% man simultaneously, without intermixture or dilution of the natures, we believe it. And we believe it *because Scripture teaches it.*

Intellectual difficulty is not necessarily a sign of doctrinal error, but rather of human incapacity. By it we are reminded of the distance between the infinite, eternal, perfect God and finite, temporal, fallen man. We are reminded of the reality of mystery in God's being. We are warned that "we are but dust" (Psa 103:14; cp. Gen 3:19; Job 34:15; Psa 104:29; Eccl 3:20; 12:7).

Morally difficult doctrines

The imputation of sin

Grudem explains the biblical perspective on Adam's fall and our condemnation: "All members of the human race were represented by Adam in the time of testing in the Garden of Eden. As our representative, Adam sinned, and God counted us guilty as well as Adam. . . . God counted Adam's guilt as belonging to us. . . . God

---

[8] Erickson, *Christian Theology*, 679, 694, 697.

[9] In Greek *hypostasis* means "being." It is the union of two words *hupo* ("under") and *stasis* ("to stand"). It means literally: "that which stands under."

rightly imputed Adam's guilt to us."[10] The Confession of Faith concurs with Grudem: Adam and Eve "being the root of all mankind, the guilt of this sin was imputed; and the same death in sin, and corrupted nature, conveyed to all their posterity descending from them by ordinary generation" (WCF 6:3).

Grudem comments on the moral revulsion to this doctrine: "When we first confront the idea that we have been counted guilty because of Adam's sin, our tendency is to protest because it seems unfair. We did not actually decide to sin, did we? Then how can we be counted guilty? Is it just for God to act this way?"[11]

Yet this understanding comes directly from Scripture:

> Until the Law sin was in the world; but sin is not imputed when there is no law. Nevertheless death reigned from Adam until Moses, even over those who had not sinned in the likeness of the offense of Adam, who is a type of Him who was to come. . . . So then as through one transgression there resulted condemnation to all men, even so through one act of righteousness there resulted justification of life to all men. For as through the one man's disobedience the many were made sinners, even so through the obedience of the One the many will be made righteous. (Rom 5:13–14, 18–19)

> For as in Adam all die, so also in Christ all shall be made alive. (1 Cor 15:22)

But if we deny the moral legitimacy of imputation, we are denying the direct biblical teaching on the subject. To make matters worse, this method ends up *destroying our own salvation*. For if it is morally inappropriate for one to act in the place of another as his representative, then it is wrong for Christ to act in our place to secure our salvation through his merit! Once again, the method-

---

[10] Grudem, *Systematic Theology*, 495.
[11] Grudem, *Systematic Theology*, 495.

ology employed to dispute predestination comes back to haunt us as Bible-believing Christians.

The exclusiveness of Christianity

The doctrine of Christian exclusivism declares that salvation only comes through Christ and his covenant and by means of a personal faith in him. In order to be saved, men must exercise faith in his name. It further teaches that no one can be saved without personally professing faith in Christ's name, no matter how "religious" they are in their devotion, how "good" they may be in their conduct, how "innocent" they may appear to others, or how "disadvantaged" is their cultural context. As the Confession states of men outside of Christ:

> much less can men, not professing the Christian religion, be saved in any other way whatsoever, be they never so diligent to frame their lives according to the light of nature, and the laws of that religion they do profess. And to assert and maintain that they may, is very pernicious, and to be detested. (WCF 10:4)

Regarding this matter, three views of salvation have arisen among theologians:

Pluralism: "A pluralist is a person who thinks humans may be saved through a number of different religious traditions and saviors."[12] On this view, all the great world religions are acceptable to God in that they arise out of man's sincere striving to find and please God. Hence, the view is "pluralistic" in that it accepts a plurality of religions.

Inclusivism: "Inclusivists believe that salvation is impossible apart from Jesus and that he is the only Savior. But this does

---

[12] Ronald H. Nash, *Is Jesus the Only Savior?* (Grand Rapids: Zondervan, 1994), 22.

not mean that people have to know about Jesus or actually believe in him to receive that salvation."[13] On this view, Jesus is the only Savior, but his salvation includes (therefore, is "inclusive") those who do not personally know him in faith.

Exclusivism: "Christian exclusivism can be defined as the belief that (1) Jesus Christ is the *only* Savior, and (2) explicit faith in Jesus Christ is necessary for salvation."[14] This is the orthodox view that is held by the vast majority of evangelical Christians.

The reasons the first two views exist at all is due to the methodological bugaboos we have been considering: emotional reflex and moral revulsion. This time the reflex is against the notion that decent people, through no fault of their own, living in non-Christian lands would be condemned by a loving, merciful God.

The inclusivist further notes that this is problematic in that God's Son died for the sins of the world. For instance, as evangelical theologian Ron Nash notes of John Hick: "Hick's encounters with devout and moral non-Christians led him to think it was no longer possible to 'argue that Christianity or Christ is the sole means of salvation since it is evident that many outside Christianity, and outside the influence of the historical Jesus, are in fact saved.'"[15]

Yet the Bible expressly and dogmatically teaches this view of salvation known as "exclusivism." This has been the historic position of the orthodox Christian church. In fact, this view underscores the *necessity* of the Christian faith and the *significance* of the Christian evangelistic and missionary outreach. Consider the following passages:

---

[13] Nash, *Is Jesus the Only Savior?*, 24

[14] Nash, *Is Jesus the Only Savior?*, 11.

[15] Cited in Nash, *Is Jesus the Only Savior?*, p. 32.

Jesus said to him, "I am the way, and the truth, and the life; no one comes to the Father, but through Me." (John 14:6)

And there is salvation in no one else; for there is no other name under heaven that has been given among men, by which we must be saved. (Acts 4:12)

For no man can lay a foundation other than the one which is laid, which is Jesus Christ. (1 Cor 3:11)

If you confess with your mouth Jesus as Lord, and believe in your heart that God raised Him from the dead, you shall be saved; for with the heart man believes, resulting in righteousness, and with the mouth he confesses, resulting in salvation . . . for 'Whoever will call upon the name of the Lord will be saved.' How then shall they call upon Him in whom they have not believed? And how shall they believe in Him whom they have not heard? And how shall they hear without a preacher? And how shall they preach unless they are sent? Just as it is written, 'How beautiful are the feet of those who bring glad tidings of good things!' (Rom 10:9–10, 13–15)

For there is one God, and one mediator also between God and men, the man Christ Jesus. (1 Tim 2:5)

So then, despite the "moral difficulty" of this historic Christian exclusivistic understanding of eternal salvation, the average evangelical Christian recognizes its necessity. Remarkably, many who oppose predestination on moral grounds will nevertheless affirm exclusivism, despite the same moral difficulty.

But now we come to the most terrifying doctrine of Scripture: the doctrine of eternal hell. So let us consider:

The eternality of hell

When we come to the doctrine of eternal hell we are entering into a discussion of the most "morally repugnant" and "emotionally repulsive" doctrine within the whole system of Christian theology.

Who can seriously contemplate the doctrine of hell without some sort of fear and trepidation? Though historically the Church has affirmed the doctrine of eternal hell, voices within the Christian tradition have long tried to re-interpret this doctrine to make it more palatable. Some have reduced the doctrine of hell to a doctrine of heck. And, of course, opponents of the Christian faith often point to the doctrine as obvious evidence that Christianity could not be true.

Influential writers expressing revulsion at the doctrine of hell include the following:

John R. W. Stott has commented (as a conservative, evangelical Christian): "Emotionally, I find the concept intolerable."[16]

Clark H. Pinnock (who deems himself evangelical) writes: "Whatever the image, the traditional understanding of hell is unspeakably horrible. How can one imagine for a moment that the God who gave his Son to die for sinners because of his great love for them would install a torture chamber somewhere in the new creation in order to subject those who reject him to everlasting pain?"[17]

Pinnock : "We are asked to believe that God endlessly tortures sinners by the million, sinners who perish because the Father has decided not to elect them to salvation [while they were alive on earth], though he could have done so, and whose torments are supposed to gladden the hearts of believers in heaven. The problems with this doctrine are both extensive and profound."[18]

Ellen G. White ("prophetess" and founder of the Seventh-day Adventist church): "How repugnant to every emotion of love and

---

[16] In David L. Edwards and John Stott, *Evangelical Essentials: A Liberal-Evangelical Dialogue* (Downers' Grove, Ill.: Inter-Varsity, 1988), 312.

[17] Pinnock, "Fire Then Nothing," in *Christianity Today* (March 20, 1987), 40.

[18] Cited in William Crockett, ed., *Four Views on Hell* (Grand Rapids: Zondervan, 1992), 136.

mercy, and even to our sense of justice, is the doctrine that the wicked dead are tormented with fire and brimstone in an eternally burning hell. . . . And how utterly revolting is the belief that as soon as the breath leaves the body the soul of the impenitent is consigned to the flames of hell!"[19]

Bertrand Russell (atheist philosopher): "There is one very serious defect to my mind in Christ's moral character, and that is that He believed in hell. I do not myself feel that any person who is really profoundly humane can believe in everlasting punishment."[20]

Nevertheless, Christians have largely agreed that the Bible teaches about hell. The following Confessional statements on hell represent the thinking of perhaps the majority of evangelical Christians:

WCF 32:1: "The souls of the wicked are cast into hell, where they remain in torments and utter darkness, reserved to the judgment of the great day."

WCF 33:2: "The end of God's appointing this day is for the manifestation of the glory of His mercy, in the eternal salvation of the elect; and of His justice, in the damnation of the reprobate, who are wicked and disobedient. For then shall the righteous go into everlasting life, and receive that fulness of joy and refreshing, which shall come from the presence of the Lord; but the wicked who know not God, and obey not the Gospel of Jesus Christ, shall be cast into eternal torments, and be punished with everlasting destruction from the presence of the Lord, and from the glory of His power."

The Bible undeniably presents eternal hell as the ultimate judgment of the wicked. In fact, more is taught about hell by Christ

---

[19] Ellen G. White, *The Great Controversy* (Oakland, Calif.: Pacific, 1887), 469, 470.

[20] Bertrand Russell, *Why I am Not a Christian* (London: Unwin, 1967), 22–23.

himself than any other single individual in Scripture. Thus, our view of hell also impacts our view of Christ and his integrity and authority, as the atheist Bertrand Russell observed. Consider the forthright declarations of Scripture — several from our Lord Jesus himself.

> You have heard that it was said, 'You shall not commit adultery'; but I say to you, that everyone who looks on a woman to lust for her has committed adultery with her already in his heart. And if your right eye makes you stumble, tear it out, and throw it from you; for it is better for you that one of the parts of your body perish, than for your whole body to be thrown into hell. And if your right hand makes you stumble, cut it off, and throw it from you; for it is better for you that one of the parts of your body perish, than for your whole body to go into hell. (Matt 5:27–30)

> So it will be at the end of the age; the angels shall come forth, and take out the wicked from among the righteous, and will cast them into the furnace of fire; there shall be weeping and gnashing of teeth. (Matt 13:49–50)

> Then He will also say to those on His left, 'Depart from Me, accursed ones, into the eternal fire which has been prepared for the devil and his angels. . . .' And these will go away into eternal punishment, but the righteous into eternal life. (Matt 25:41, 46)

> And whoever causes one of these little ones who believe to stumble, it would be better for him if, with a heavy millstone hung around his neck, he had been cast into the sea. And if your hand causes you to stumble, cut it off; it is better for you to enter life crippled, than having your two hands, to go into hell, into the unquenchable fire, where their worm does not die, and the fire is not quenched. And if your foot causes you to stumble, cut it off; it is better for you to enter life lame, than having your two feet, to be cast into hell, where their worm does not die, and the fire is not quenched. And if your eye causes you to stumble, cast it out; it is better for you to enter the kingdom of God with one

eye, than having two eyes, to be cast into hell, where their worm does not die, and the fire is not quenched.' (Mark 9:42–48)

Just as Sodom and Gomorrah and the cities around them, since they in the same way as these indulged in gross immorality and went after strange flesh, are exhibited as an example, in undergoing the punishment of eternal fire. (Jude 7)

And another angel, a third one, followed them, saying with a loud voice, 'If anyone worships the beast and his image, and receives a mark on his forehead or upon his hand, he also will drink of the wine of the wrath of God, which is mixed in full strength in the cup of His anger; and he will be tormented with fire and brimstone in the presence of the holy angels and in the presence of the Lamb. And the smoke of their torment goes up forever and ever; and they have no rest day and night, those who worship the beast and his image, and whoever receives the mark of his name.' (Rev 14:9–11)

According to a recent Gallup Poll (2015), 58% of the American population believes in hell, whereas 82% of evangelical Protestants believe in hell (hopefully not because their church service is so bad).[21] The average evangelical Christian accepts the doctrine of hell, despite its intellectual and moral challenges. Yet many of the same Christians reject predestination on identical intellectual and moral grounds. This exposes inconsistency in one's reasoning. We must accept what the Scripture teaches no matter how difficult it may seem to our finite, fallen conceptions.

May I question God?

The previous study demonstrates inconsistencies in the *thought patterns* of many evangelicals. If we can reject a doctrine such as

---

[21] Carlyle Murphy, "Most Americans believe in heaven and hell," (Pew Research Center, Nov. 10, 2015). www.Pewresearch.org/fact-takn/s015/11/10most-Americans-believe-in-heaven-and-hell

predestination because it either perplexes us intellectually or is contrary to our moral sensitivities, then consistency should require our rejecting other similarly difficult doctrines. Our study should cause us to recognize *unbiblical assumptions* in our thinking, assumptions that contradict our view of God (as infinite and eternal) and our view of man (as finite and fallen) — and our view of Scripture (as inerrant and authoritative).

> O Lord, what is man, that You take knowledge of him? / Or the son of man, that You think of him? / *Man is like a mere breath; / His days are like a passing shadow*. (Psa 144:3–4)

> Around God is *awesome majesty*. / The Almighty — we cannot find Him; / He is *exalted in power*. (Job 37:22b–23a)

> He is the blessed and only Sovereign, the King of kings and Lord of lords; who alone possesses immortality and dwells in unapproachable light; whom no man has seen or can see. To Him be honor and eternal dominion! Amen. (1 Tim 6:15–16)

> Who has measured the waters in the hollow of His hand, / And marked off the heavens by the span, / And calculated the dust of the earth by the measure, / And weighed the mountains in a balance, / And the hills in a pair of scales? / Who has directed the Spirit of the Lord, / Or as His counselor has informed Him? / With whom did He consult and who gave Him understanding? / And who taught Him in the path of justice and taught Him knowledge, / And informed Him of the way of understanding? (Isa 40:12–14)

This study of theological method should encourage us as we explain the doctrine of God's absolute sovereignty in predestination, as well as provide for us a means of responding to various objections against this mystifying doctrine (see next chapter).

In addition to our theological method, we must consider another issue: Before we challenge a doctrine that is not congenial to our times or in keeping with our expectations, we must ask: "Who am I to challenge God's word?" We must ask this since: (1) we do recognize God's eternal existence, infinite presence, almighty power and perfect moral rectitude, and (2) we confess that we are but temporal creatures of dust, limited and frail in our being, and sinfully rebellious in our nature and thinking: How shall we stand and argue against God? Consider the following samples from Scripture.

The Book of Job

In Job's encounter with God, Job learns that man must not question God. God confronts him with this truth by letting him know of the infinite distance between them. We see this in the words of Job's friends, Job himself, and God:

> How long will you say these things, / and the words of your mouth be a mighty wind? Does God pervert justice / Or does the Almighty pervert what is right? (Job 8:2–3)

> In truth I know that this is so, / But how can a man be in the right before God? / If one wished to dispute with Him, / he could not answer Him once in a thousand times. / Wise in heart and mighty in strength, / Who has defied Him without harm? / It is God who removes the mountains, / they know not how, / When He overturns them in His anger; / Who shakes the earth out of its place, And its pillars tremble; / Who commands the sun not to shine, / And sets a seal upon the stars; / Who alone stretches out the heavens, / And tramples down the waves of the sea. (Job 9:2–8)

> Behold, let me tell you, you are not right in this, / for God is greater than man. / Why do you complain against Him, / That He does not give an account of all His doings? (Job 33:12–13)

> Then the Lord answered Job out of the whirlwind and said, / Who is this that darkens counsel / By words without knowledge? / Now gird up your loins like a man, / And I will ask you, and you

instruct Me! / Where were you when I laid the foundation of the earth? / Tell Me, if you have understanding, / Who set its measurements, since you know? / Or who stretched the line on it? (Job 38:1–5)

All flesh is grass, and all its loveliness is like the flower of the field. / The grass withers, the flower fades, / When the breath of the Lord blows upon it; / Surely the people are grass. / The grass withers, the flower fades, / But the word of our God stands forever. / Get yourself up on a high mountain, / O Zion, bearer of good news, / Lift up your voice mightily, / O Jerusalem, bearer of good news; / Lift it up, do not fear. / Say to the cities of Judah, 'Here is your God!' / Behold, the Lord God will come with might, / With His arm ruling for Him. / Behold, His reward is with Him, / And His recompense before Him. (Job 40:6–10)

Who has given to Me that I should repay him? / Whatever is under the whole heaven is Mine. (Job 41:11)

Job said to God: 'I know that You can do all things, / And that no purpose of Yours can be thwarted. / Who is this that hides counsel without knowledge? / Therefore I have declared that which I did not understand, / Things too wonderful for me, which I did not know. / Hear, now, and I will speak; / I will ask You and You instruct me. / I have heard of You by the hearing of the ear; / But now my eye sees You; / Therefore I retract, / And I repent in dust and ashes.' (Job 42:2–6)

The Prophets

The prophets also warn against the meager creature's replying against the majestic Creator. This has been a problem from the beginning (Gen 3:1–6). For example, we see this in two of the major prophets, Isaiah and Jeremiah:

Woe to the one who quarrels with his Maker — / An earthenware vessel among the vessels of earth! / *Will the clay say to the potter,*

"*What are you doing?*" / Or the thing you are making say, "He has no hands"? (Isa 45:9)

Then the word of the Lord came to me saying, "*Can I not, O house of Israel, deal with you as this potter does?*" declares the Lord. "Behold, like the clay in the potter's hand, so are you in My hand, O house of Israel. At one moment I might speak concerning a nation or concerning a kingdom to uproot, to pull down, or to destroy it. (Jer 18:5–7)

The New Testament

Later we will look more closely at Paul's specific response to creaturely objections against God's sovereignty. But now we just note that the New Testament does *directly confront* such objections:

Just as it is written, "Jacob I loved, but Esau I hated." What shall we say then? There is no injustice with God, is there? May it never be! For He says to Moses, "I will have mercy on whom I have mercy, and I will have compassion on whom I have compassion." So then it does not depend on the man who wills or the man who runs, but on God who has mercy. For the Scripture says to Pharaoh, "For this very purpose I raised you up, to demonstrate My power in you, and that My name might be proclaimed throughout the whole earth." So then He has mercy on whom He desires, and He hardens whom He desires. You will say to me then, "Why does He still find fault? For who resists His will?" On the contrary, *who are you, O man, who answers back to God?* The thing molded will not say to the molder, "Why did you make me like this," will it? Or does not the potter have a right over the clay, to make from the same lump one vessel for honorable use, and another for common use? What if God, although willing to demonstrate His wrath and to make His power known, endured with much patience vessels of wrath prepared for destruction? (Rom 9:13–22)

Conclusion

Having presented and defended the doctrine of predestination, we must emphasize our need for consistency. Evangelicals hold several doctrines that are intellectually incomprehensible (the Trinity, the two natures of Christ) and morally repugnant (hell, Christian exclusivism). Yet many deny the doctrine of predestination on these very grounds. Christians need to carefully think through the problem of method and the issue of consistency.

Furthermore, we must bow in humility before God's majesty at all times. How can we dare challenge a doctrine simply because we cannot comprehend it? Is not God exalted above us so that we must recognize him as the potter and ourselves as the clay? That is, can we allow our creaturely confusion to discount a perplexing doctrine simply because it is perplexing? Surely we must humbly submit to God in all of life, even with our intellects. We must, as Paul urges, take "every thought captive to the obedience of Christ" (2 Cor 10:5b). After all, God himself informs us: "My ways are higher than your ways / And My thoughts than your thoughts" (Isa 55:9).

As demanded by all we have seen, only predestination's biblical status should sway our thinking. After all, Scripture "is inspired by God and profitable for teaching, for reproof, for correction, for training in righteousness; that the man of God may be adequate, equipped for every good work" (2 Tim. 3:16–17) — no matter how difficult its teaching may be.

Chapter 8
ANSWERING THE OBJECTIONS

In this chapter I will quickly gather and summarize the responses to a few arguments that I have touched on previously, and provide a few supporting verses. Then I will focus more closely on some additional objections frequently brought against the doctrine of predestination.

Previous Objections Reviewed

"Predestination is not a biblical doctrine"

I have shown that the doctrine is very much a biblical doctrine. The words "election" and "predestination" are even biblical terms. God's absolute sovereignty either appears on or is implied on almost every page of Scripture. We very definitely see the doctrine in such verses as the following:

> For truly in this city there were gathered together against Your holy servant Jesus, whom You anointed, both Herod and Pontius Pilate, along with the Gentiles and the peoples of Israel, to do whatever Your hand and Your purpose predestined to occur. (Acts 4:27-28)

> We have obtained an inheritance, having been predestined according to His purpose who works all things after the counsel of His will. (Eph 1:11)

"The doctrine of predestination is incomprehensible"

We must understand that our *comprehension* of God's ways is not required; only our *faith* in his word is. The attitude of the man who comes to Jesus must be ours: "I do believe; help my unbelief" (Mark

9:24). We should expect mystery in the things of God because of his infinite, eternal, and holy nature and our finite, temporal, and fallen condition. After all, who can understand the Trinitarian being of God, or his eternity? Or the two natures of Christ in one person? The Bible warns us of this problem:

> "My thoughts are not your thoughts, / Neither are your ways My ways," declares the Lord. / "For as the heavens are higher than the earth, / So are My ways higher than your ways, / And My thoughts than your thoughts." (Isa 55:8–9)

> Can you discover the depths of God? / Can you discover the limits of the Almighty? (Job 11:7)

> Oh, the depth of the riches both of the wisdom and knowledge of God! How unsearchable are His judgments and unfathomable His ways! (Rom 11:33)

"Predestination is morally repugnant"

Our moral guidance must be from God's word, not from our own sympathies. In fact, the "moral repugnance" problem is not unique to predestination, it arises regarding a host of evangelical doctrines, such as Christian exclusivism (salvation comes only in Christianity) and eternal hell (God condemns some people to unending, conscious torment). In this regard, consider these statements from Scripture:

> Then the Lord said to Job, / "Will the faultfinder contend with the Almighty? / Let him who reproves God answer it." (Job 40:1-2)

> You will say to me then, "Why does He still find fault? For who resists His will?" On the contrary, who are you, O man, who answers back to God? The thing molded will not say to the molder, "Why did you make me like this," will it? Or does not the potter have a right over the clay, to make from the same lump one vessel for honorable use, and another for common use? (Rom 9:19–21)

But let us now consider some other common complaints against this difficult doctrine. These are frequently experienced in print, in the pulpit, and in person. Perhaps you are even a predestinarian but have wondered about these issues yourself. Handling these should help you in both defending and understanding the doctrine.

New Objections Considered

"Predestination is based on foreknowledge"

Many opponents of predestination argue that the doctrine does not teach that God sovereignly determines in eternity past to save sinners. Rather, it really means only that God determines to save men whom he sees in advance will respond to the gospel. Thus, predestination is really just God's advance confirmation of the sinner's eventual response to his call. Predestination is rooted in God's foreknowledge of the future.

This is probably the most popular evangelical response to absolute predestination. Non-Calvinist Christians think that foreknowledge removes the onus of determinism, while preserving God's omniscience, power, and grace. But this actually fails to help, for several reasons.

First, foreknowledge in itself entails certainty. And this absolute certainty effectively undermines the freedom that the objector seeks to defend. If from eternity past God perfectly knows all things that will transpire in history, then are not those things absolutely sure and unchangeable *regardless of our actions*? Are not our actions thus fixed and sure? Thus, even God's mere foreknowledge presents a problem to the objector.

Second, simple foreknowledge removes control from God. If we object to predestination and attempt to deny it in favor of mere prescience, then another serious problem arises. In this view, God merely witnesses in advance the factors leading to man's actions. He does not plan nor does he intervene in history so as to cause people to move one way or another. Rather, man's actions are left under the control of his will, his culture, the environment, chemistry, biology, chance, and other non-personalistic factors. This removes God from active participation in the Universe and makes him simply a spectator. This is much like the Deistic view of God which argues that the Universe is like a clock that God creates, winds up, and lets run on its own. This simply is not the picture of God which Scripture presents.

In fact, one contemporary anti-predestinarian, reinterpretation of God's sovereignty even challenges his omniscience, partly out of concern for "true freedom." These "Openness of God" theologians, such as Clark Pinnock and John Saunders, teach that the future is unknowable *even to God*. This is because future history depends on an infinite variety of interacting and contingent variables regarding the uncertain future actions of men with free will. In their view, the future is altogether "open" and unknowable. This is a high price to pay for objecting to predestination. Yet it logically follows upon concerns such as expressed in this problem with the doctrine.

This also makes prophecy *as presented in Scripture* impossible. If God only sees what is going to happen in the future, then things which transpire do so because of forces *outside of himself.* Prophecy becomes passive, rather than active, for God does not cause those events. Consequently, prophecy can have no effect on the direction of history; prophecy becomes only a foreview of the inevitable. Yet Scripture presents prophecy as history-altering, not history-previewing:

> The Lord of hosts has sworn saying, 'Surely, just as I have intended so it has happened, and just as I have planned so it will stand.' (Isa 14:24)

> Have you not heard? / Long ago I did it, / From ancient times I planned it. / Now I have brought it to pass, / That you should turn fortified cities into ruinous heaps. (Isa 37:26)

Truly I have spoken; truly I will bring it to pass. / I have planned it, surely I will do it. (Isa 46:11)

Therefore hear the plan of the Lord which He has planned against Babylon, and His purposes which He has purposed against the land of the Chaldeans: surely they will drag them off, even the little ones of the flock; surely He will make their pasture desolate because of them. (Jer 50:45)

"Predestination conflicts with free will"

The problem of free will is a quite familiar objection presented against the doctrine of predestination. The objector points out that we cannot hold both to free-will and predestination in that they are logically incompatible and are contrary to the biblical presentation of man as a free moral agent. If God predetermines man's actions, then man becomes a puppet lacking free will, an automaton without self-determination or true significance.

Even the Calvinist might wonder how he did it, but we must never think we are like Howdy Doody. In responding to this objection, we must begin by defining what we mean by "free will." This is important in that the concept is used in different ways.

Defining free will

Specifically for our purposes, we must distinguish between man's metaphysical will and his moral will. Calvinists do, in fact, believe that men make genuine, free choices; we accept *metaphysical* free will. That is, man's will is truly free and is not *coerced* by God so as to destroy his freedom. But man lacks *moral* free will because he is *constrained* by his own indwelling sin which prohibits him from choosing to do that which is truly good in the eyes of God. Scripture is clear regarding man's lacking *moral* free will:

For while we were in the flesh, the sinful passions, which were
aroused by the Law, were at work in the members of our body to
bear fruit for death. (Rom 7:5)

Those who are in the flesh cannot please God. (Rom 8:8)

And you were dead in your trespasses and sins . . . and were by
nature children of wrath. (Eph 2:1, 3)

You were dead in your transgressions. (Col 2:13)

So then, *morally* man is *not* free — due to his own fallen nature.
But *metaphysically* he is free — in that no external force compels his
actions against his own free self-determination. Morally every sinful
choice man makes is a genuine choice from within his own will,
even though constrained by his own sin. Metaphysically man's will
is free.

To illustrate this conundrum, let us consider a mundane matter:
Calvinism teaches that God foreordains my choice to eat pizza.
Nevertheless, it is *my* choice which God has ordained. That is, God
does not simply foreordain my eating pizza, so that by his will I
simply go through the mechanical muscular actions of physically
securing a slice of pizza, manually ingesting it into my mouth,
masticating it by repeated strokes of the mandible, then swallowing
it through the gastroesophageal sphincter. Rather he foreordains
even my *choosing* to eat pizza.

Perhaps an issue regarding Christ on earth can illustrate the
matter for us. Take the case of Christ's bones. He was truly and fully
human. Consequently, his bones were common, human bones by
their very God created nature. God, however, foreordained that not
one of his bones would be broken (Psa 34:20; John 19:36). Despite
the God-ordained impossibility of their breaking, his bones remained by their very nature a collagen-rich organic matrix impreg-
nated with calcium, phosphate, magnesium, potassium, and other
minerals — and as porous, semi-rigid material they were fragile.
They did not differ from our bones; they were not made of

hardened, tempered steel. Likewise man's will is metaphysically free so that he may, if he chooses, do good (like Christ's bones were free to break). Yet man outside of Christ cannot choose good because his own fallen nature compels him to sin (like Christ's bones were not able to break).

Thus, man's acts *in themselves* are contingent (dependent upon circumstances), open (capable of alternative directions), and free (not controlled by external forces). That is the inherent nature of the God-created thing. But in terms of God's plan, those actions are determined and certain. The problem confounds us due to our failure to maintain the balance of two perspectives: the earthly perspective and the eternal perspective. Yet our worldview demands a two-level reality: the Creator and creation, the uncreated God and the created cosmos. As Calvin points out in his *Institutes of the Christian Religion*:

> What God has determined must necessarily so take place even though it is neither unconditionally nor of its own peculiar nature necessary. There is something which is not necessary to happen but which must necessarily take place because of God's plan.

Though this is intellectually perplexing, we must remember that our reason is not the limit of God's ability.

Understanding Free Will

When speaking of free will much confusion arises in describing it. Some of the following descriptions are especially popular:

1. "Free will involves the voluntary action of the agent, an action that is not compelled."

This assertion is true, and does not contradict the Calvinist conception of predestination. We should remember our earlier discussion noting that God does not force man's will, otherwise we would have to say man does not have a free will in any sense. If man's will were forced, then he could not be responsible for his actions and could not be subject to God's judging him.

By way of illustration we should note God's absolute predetermination in ordaining Judas' betraying Christ and then parallels that with the equally strong biblical assertion that he was responsible for that predetermined betrayal:

> The Son of man goeth *as it is written* of him: but *woe unto that man* by whom the Son of man is betrayed! it had been good for that man if he had not been born. (Matt 26:24)

> Judas said: "*I have sinned* in that *I have betrayed* the innocent blood." (Matt 27:4)

Judas possessed metaphysical free will and was therefore responsible, even though he acted in terms of God's predetermined plan. And he knew that he was responsible.

Scripture affirms man's responsibility. For instance, in Deuteronomy 30:19 we read: "I call heaven and earth to witness against you today, that I have set before you life and death, the blessing and the curse. So choose life in order that you may live, you and your descendants." This definition of free will as "a voluntary action that is not compelled" simply shows that man has a will. It is virtually true by definition — and acceptable in the Calvinist scheme. Simply put, Calvinists *do* believe in free will, while simultaneously believing in predestination.

2. "The choices we make are determined, but are limited by our own internal character."

This recognizes the distinction between metaphysical free will and moral free will, and also adequately represents the matter. Scripture frequently teaches that the kind of person we are determines the choices we make.

> For out of the heart come evil thoughts, murders, adulteries, fornications, thefts, false witness, slanders. (Matt 15:19)

> But each one is tempted when he is carried away and enticed by his own lust. Then when lust has conceived, it gives birth to sin; and when sin is accomplished, it brings forth death. (Jms 1:14–15)

We make our own choices according to our internal character. As our Lord puts it: "a bad tree will not bear good fruit" (Matt 7:17). We are metaphysically free even though our actions are determined by our own moral character and constrained by our fallen abilities.

No one believes that man's will is *absolutely* free, so that I could freely decide I will float to the moon, expecting that it will happen because I freely willed it. Nor that a human can act in terms of the nature of an accordion, simply because his will is free. If such a definition of free will were true, then we could never trust anyone because we could never predict their conduct based on their character. They would be absolutely free of any constraints, even internal character constraints. Absolute freedom leads to absolute unpredictability, wherein we would have no way to know how one might act under any set of conditions.

We do not believe that our will is independent of our character. The kind of person I am determines the choices I make. Our foundational character controls our willful acts. The Scriptures clearly teach this.

I make my own choices according to my internal character; I am metaphysically free but my actions are determined by my moral character. In fact, as Boettner notes, a man "is limited by the laws of the physical world, by his particular environment, habits, past training, social customs, fear of punishment or disapproval, his present desires, ambitions, etc., so that he is far from being the absolute master of his actions."[1]

---

[1] Boettner, *Reformed Doctrine of Predestination*, 221.

Consider the circumstances of the spirits of the righteous, who are already in heaven, and of ourselves when we finally receive our resurrection bodies. These will have free will in the biblical sense. Nevertheless, none from either of these classes is (or will be) capable of choosing to do evil. Otherwise, they could fall from heaven and be lost. Yet no reasonable evangelical complains that these have no free will because it is impossible that these people should sin in those estates.

3. "We must be able to choose independently of God's decree, otherwise our actions are not voluntary actions."

This is a false concept. This view is widely held by Christians, thereby causing problems for understanding the biblical doctrine of predestination. It affirms some biblical teachings while denying others. It is a half-truth which is biblically unbalanced. The problem with a half-truth is that not only do you not know which half you have, but it's twice as hard to crush a half-truth as a whole lie.

The Bible teaches both that our choices are determined by God's predestinating will, but are not compelled by God's forcing us to do something we do not want to do. The complaint arises: "How does God do that?" In answering this conundrum I am like Mark Twain who once stated the following about a reporter's question to him: "I was gratified to be able to answer promptly. I said I don't know." We do not know for God has not told us. This is not a question of *logic*, but of metaphysics.

We do not know *how* God created the universe, parted the Red Sea, caused Joshua's long day, and so forth. We do not understand God's eternality or omnipresence, but these attributes are real. God can do all things; man cannot. All we can do is admit "with men this is impossible, but with God all things are possible" (Matt 19:26). But God is not limited by our scope of understanding. The problem is that we tend to think of God in human terms, as if he were on our level. But this is contrary to biblical teaching. In the final analysis,

Boettner well illustrates the matter: "Predestination and free agency are the twin pillars of a great temple, and they meet above the clouds where the human gaze cannot penetrate."[2]

The "problem" of predestination and free-will must be resolved from the source of our theological knowledge. If the Bible is our authority, then we must accept what it teaches, regardless of our human capacity to understand it. If our source of authority is something other than the Bible, then we are not reasoning in a truly Christian manner.

God's predetermination makes an event certain, but it also insures personal responsibility on the creature's part. God determines, but I freely act. There is no *logical* contradiction inherent in this. It is simply a great mystery. Paul does not even consider the "problem" of free will, nor does he shrink from his strong assertion on predetermination:

> You will say to me then, "Why does He still find fault? For who resists His will?" On the contrary, who are you, O man, who answers back to God? The thing molded will not say to the molder, "Why did you make me like this," will it? (Rom 9:19–20)

This passage reminds us that though God's word asserts both God's absolute sovereignty and man's free agency, it nowhere attempts to reconcile the two for us.

According to biblical teaching we choose because of God's predestinating will, but not by *compulsion* from him. This confounds us in that we cannot see how God can do that. But we must remember that God is not limited by our abilities or our capacity of understanding. Once again we must consider the following biblical statements:

> "For My thoughts are not your thoughts, / Neither are your ways My ways," declares the Lord. / "For as the heavens are higher

---

[2] Boettner, *Reformed Doctrine of Predestination*, 222.

than the earth, / So are My ways higher than your ways, / And My thoughts than your thoughts." (Isa 55:8–9)

Can you discover the depths of God? / Can you discover the limits of the Almighty? (Job 11:7)

Do you hear the secret counsel of God, / And limit wisdom to yourself? (Job 15:8)

Oh, the depth of the riches both of the wisdom and knowledge of God! How unsearchable are His judgments and unfathomable His ways! (Rom 11:33)

We simply must avoid the tendency to think of God in human terms, as if he were on our level. This is contrary to biblical thinking. If I as a human determine that some decent person should rob a bank for me, I have to override his free will through some sort of psychoactive drugs, psychic hypnosis, terrifying threats, or physical force of some kind. But God does not have to do such. For me to determine someone's action requires that I work against their free will through some sort of coercive stratagem, but God does not have to do it thus. As noted previously he exists on a different plane of being, the eternal, whereas I exist in the temporal world. God exists above and beyond us, whereas we exist "across the table" from each other. We simply cannot understand how God's eternal being causes earthly events without his overriding secondary causes. But Scripture teaches that he does.

God's predetermination makes an event certain, but it also insures personal responsibility on the creature's part. God determines, but I freely act. There is no *logical* contradiction inherent in this. It is simply a great mystery. When God predestines an event, he does not change the true character of the thing predestined nor does he dismiss secondary causes. He does not change man's true significance, personality, or will to get his predetermined end accomplished. Again, it is like the prophecy that not one bone of Jesus shall be broken. This did not imply that Jesus's bones were made of steel. They were still fragile, human bones. But under no circumstances could they break.

Since God uses secondary causes and means to effect his will, he ordains the free moral agency of man to effect his own will. Thus, my free will is a fixed consideration ordained by God. The Confession of Faith well captures the biblical reality:

> God from all eternity, did, by the most wise and holy counsel of His own will, freely, and unchangeably ordain whatsoever comes to pass; yet so, as thereby neither is God the author of sin, nor is violence offered to the will of the creatures; nor is the liberty or contingency of second causes taken away, but rather established. (WCF 3:1)

The objector to the Calvinistic doctrine must be careful that he not wrongly explain our view. We insist that predestination and free-will operate concurrently, that both are true. After all, the Bible teaches us that "a man's heart devises his way; but the Lord directs his steps" (Prov 16:9).

Regarding God's plan and predestination on the issue of contingent events, Calvin taught that: (1) The thing in itself is contingent, open, susceptible to change. That is the nature of the God-created thing. (2) But in terms of God's plan it is determined and absolutely certain. That is the revealed truth of God's absolute sovereignty.

Anyone who believes in biblical prophecy must recognize the compatibility of sovereignty and freedom, whether they understand it or not. Was it true that the soldiers crucified Christ? Did the Bible prophesy this would happen? Was it absolutely certain to occur? Was it in God's plan? Now then: Did the soldiers have the *ability* to do otherwise? What of Pilate? Was he coerced? Or did he (and the soldiers) do it by "wicked hands" as they chose?

"Predestination makes God the author of sin"

This objection frequently arises against God's absolute sovereignty in predestination, and is a perfectly understandable concern. Scripture clearly teaches that God is not the author of sin: "Let no one say when he is tempted, 'I am being tempted by God'; for God cannot be tempted by evil, and He Himself does not tempt anyone" (Jms 1:13). This is because God is "not a God who takes pleasure in wickedness; / No evil dwells with Thee" (Psa 5:4). "The Lord is upright; / He is my rock, and there is no unrighteousness in Him" (Psa 92:15). "There is no injustice with God, is there? May it never be!" (Rom 9:14).

Nevertheless, this objection cannot overthrow the doctrine of God's absolute sovereignty for the following reasons.

First, this complaint is another instance of the problem that always faces us simply because our minds are unable to relate God's sovereignty and man's free will. This new problem of understanding the reality of sin and the ultimate responsibility for it is answered in the same way as the previous one. We simply cannot understand how God can ordain the sinful acts of men and yet not be the author of the sin involved. Yet that is precisely what the Bible teaches.

Thus, once again we are confronted with mystery in God. If we denied any and all mystery in our conception of God, we would be affirming that the infinite, eternal, all-holy, exalted God is fully comprehensible to finite, temporal, fallen, earth-bound man. We would, in effect, have a God different from the God of the Bible. God's ways and thoughts are necessarily higher than ours (Isa 55:8–9).

Second, this problem involving divine sovereignty and human sin is not unique to the issues of predestination and sovereignty. It confronts us when we consider even the more generally accepted issues of predictive prophecy and divine omniscience. Many prophecies of Scripture infallibly prophesy some evil action (e.g., the ruthless invasion of Israel by the Babylonians, the crucifixion of Christ, his betrayal by Judas, and so forth). Yet the evangelical does not hold that God is responsible for the sinful actions that are certain because they were ordained in prophecy. For instance, in Acts 3:18 we read: "But the things which God announced before-hand by the mouth of all the prophets, that His Christ should suffer, He has thus fulfilled." In fact, in Luke 22:22 we read: "For indeed, the Son of Man is going as it has been determined; but woe to that man by whom He is betrayed!" So then, just as prophecy and free will are compatible without implicating God in sin, so is God's sovereignty and man's sinning.

Third, anyone who holds even that God *knows* all things before they happen confronts the same moral objection. After all, on this type of complaint if God creates a man while fully knowing he will do evil (e.g., Nero, Hitler, or Stalin), is God himself not responsible for the evil that results from his creative work? If I give a loaded handgun to a three year old in a crowded nursery, am I not responsible for any resulting injury or death that occurs? But again, this is looking at the problem one dimensionally, "on the same plane" or "across the board," rather than looking across two planes of existence: the eternal and the temporal.

We know that sin was involved in God's plan from before the foundation of the world — whether by divine prescience or by divine decree. For we read in Scripture that we are redeemed "with precious blood, as of a lamb unblemished and spotless, the blood of Christ" who "was foreknown *before* the *foundation of the world*" (1 Pet 1:19–20). His incarnation as "Christ" the Redeemer would not have been necessary had man not fallen. Yet "before the foundation of the world" this very "Christ" was foreknown. In fact, the wisdom involved in the work of redemption "was in accordance with the *eternal* purpose which He carried out in Christ Jesus our Lord" (Col 3:11).

Yet we know that the motive man has in committing sin fundamentally differs from God's motive in ordaining (*not* causing) it. We may rest assured — based on divine revelation in Scripture — that God has a good and sufficient reason for ordaining sin's entrance into the world.

As we have noted before, in many places in Scripture we see God using sin to bring about good. For instance, when Joseph was wickedly sold into slavery by his brothers, Joseph interprets the situation thus: "as for you, you meant evil against me, but God meant it for good in order to bring about this present result, to preserve many people alive" (Gen 50:20). God raised up Pharaoh for the purpose of bringing glory to himself: "And as for Me, behold, I will harden the hearts of the Egyptians so that they will go in [the Red Sea] after them; and I will be honored through Pharaoh and all his army, through his chariots and his horsemen" (Exo 14:17).

Fourth, if we allow the alternative to the Calvinist scheme, we would be cast into utter despair and abject hopelessness. For then on that basis, God created the world and did not ordain sin, *yet sin nevertheless invaded and corrupted his creation against his will!* The alternative is depressing, for in such a situation we are subject to random forces beyond God's control.

In the final analysis we must "let God be true and every man a liar" (Rom 3:4) in that Scripture teaches that God "works *all things* after the counsel of His will*" (Eph 1:11) — *all* things, including evil. God declares "the end from the beginning and from ancient times things which have not been done, Saying, '*My purpose will be established*, And *I will accomplish all My good pleasure*'" (Isa 46:10) — even in a world of sin.

"Evil and sovereignty destroy the idea of God"

This problem involves one of our foremost challenges as Christians who want to defend the faith: the existence of sin and suffering in a God-created, God-governed world. Atheists have long argued that "The Problem of Evil" is a compelling argument that logically destroys the very notion of the Christian God. The Christian response to this problem is known as "theodicy" (*theos* = "God"; *dike* = "justice"), that is, the "vindication of God" in light of the existence of evil and suffering.

The "problem of evil" argument follows this general pattern of reasoning:

1. The Christian claims God is both perfectly good and infinitely powerful.
2. But sin and suffering exist in the world.
3. So then, either:
   a. God is not all-good (in that he allows sin and suffering), or
   b. he his not all-powerful (because he is not able to prevent sin and suffering).
4. Therefore, the all-good, all-powerful God of Christianity cannot exist.

Some theists, such as Jewish Rabbi Harold S. Kushner (author of *When Bad Things Happen to Good People*), have developed a theology that attempts to resolve this problem. Kushner states that though God is all good, he is not all powerful. God is immensely powerful, to be sure, but he is not omnipotently sovereign. Therefore, the reason bad things happen in the world is because God is not all powerful. This, of course, will not suffice for the evangelical, Bible-based Christian.

Despite the atheist challenge, the problem fails to highlight a *logical* contradiction in the notion of God. The nature of the "problem" the unbeliever confronts us with is supposedly a logical incompatibility of an all good, all powerful God existing, where evil and suffering also exist. This fails as a logical argument against God for the following reasons:

First, the existence of an all good, all powerful God is not *logically* incompatible with the existence of sin and suffering. Despite its presentation as such, this is not a *logical* problem, at all. Stating that something is both "A" and not "A" would be a logical contradiction. But stating that an all good and all powerful God exists and sin and suffering exist is not *logically* incompatible.

Second, this "problem" as presented against the existence of God assumes God does not have a morally sufficient reason for allowing evil. But you cannot prove or justify a universal negative. That is, you cannot prove that *no* sufficient moral reason exists *anywhere* in the Universe. You may be able to discount a hundred arguments, or a thousand, or a million, but you cannot disprove an infinite number of arguments. You cannot defend a universal negative on the basis of human reason.

The Scriptures repeatedly demonstrate that God brings good out of evil, as in Genesis 50:20: "And as for you, you meant evil against me, but God meant it for good in order to bring about this present result, to preserve many people alive." We see this in other such passages, such as Exodus 9:16; 10:1–2; 11:9; Numbers 24:10; Nehemiah 13:2; John 11:4; Philippians 1:12; and Hebrews 12:11. We may reasonably suppose, therefore, that this is true across the board — even though *we* ourselves cannot always discern the good from *our* perspective.

God's allowing evil is something like a parent who puts his racoon-bitten child through painful rabies shots for morally sufficient reasons. The goodness of God is the measure of good, not the goodness of man. There may be a reason for evil which we do not know. In fact, we do believe God has morally sufficient reasons, even though he has not revealed those to us.

Third, the atheist challenge to the Christian view of God fails also in that the unbelieving system does not have the basic assumptions or the intellectual preconditions necessary for distinguishing between good and evil. In the unbelieving worldview, all is relative, all is in a state of flux. Consequently, there can be no absolutes. The unbeliever cannot say absolutely: "This is evil or that is evil."

Good and evil requires absolute standards for evaluation, therefore the notions of good and evil cannot exist apart from the foundation of the Christian worldview. Thus, the atheist challenge is incoherent when it disclaims the presence of evil because they have no way to define good and evil.

Ironically, evil arose just because man questions God! This is why evil exists in the first place as we see in Gen 3:1. The nature of the problem points to the solution: If Adam and Eve had not questioned God, there would be no evil. We assume the attitude of fallen man, rather than trusting in God when we cower at the problem of evil.

We may wonder how Adam and Eve (who were created good) made an evil decision. But we do not know why. In fact, by the very nature of the case Adam's decision was irrational, therefore we cannot discern a rational answer. But we know it was in the plan of God, because our redemption was planned from before the foundation of the world (Eph 1:4–5; 3:11; 2 Tim 1:9; 1 Pet 1:20; Rev 17:8).

"Predestination forbids those who want to be saved"

Some objectors point out that Jesus preaches a free offer of the gospel: "Come to Me, all who are weary and heavy-laden, and I will give you rest" (Matt 11:28). They note that Peter declares to an open audience at Pentecost: "'Repent, and let each of you be baptized in the name of Jesus Christ for the forgiveness of your sins; and you shall receive the gift of the Holy Spirit. . . .' And with many other words he solemnly testified and kept on exhorting them, saying, 'Be saved from this perverse generation!'" (Acts 2:38, 40). Yet, they argue, if predestination were true it would forbid such free offers of the gospel and preclude the non-elect from coming to Christ.

This objection arises from a radical misconception regarding the Calvinist doctrine of salvation. No Bible-believing predestinarian teaches that God prohibits seekers from coming to Christ or forbids their being accepted by him when they reach out to him. Interestingly, some of the greatest missionaries and evangelists in Christian history have been firm Calvinists. We can name such luminaries as the renowned Great Awakening revivalists, Jonathan Edwards (1703–58) and George Whitefield (1714 –70), as well as "the father of modern missions," William Carey (1761 –1834), and the "Prince of Preachers," C. H. Spurgeon (1834–92). Indeed, Roger S. Greenway well notes in the *Evangelical Dictionary of World Missions*: "Historically, Calvinism has played a major role in the Protestant mission enterprise over the past two centuries. A large percentage, in some cases the majority, of missionaries serving in parts of Africa, Asia, and Latin America have been Calvinists."[3]

Actually God's sovereignty makes it possible for sinners to come to Christ. Once again, the objector overlooks the disabling and destructive power of sin. Apart from God's sovereign calling *no one* would seek after God. The Scripture plainly declares that "there is none who understands, there is none who seeks for God" (Rom 3:11). This is because outside of Christ men are "dead in trespasses and sins" (Eph 2:1, 5; cp. Col 2:13). Consequently, the Lord himself states that "no one *can* come to Me, *unless* the Father who sent Me draws him; and I will raise him up on the last day" (John 6:44). This is much like the situation with dead Lazarus. On his own he could not arise out of the grave and come to Christ. But when the powerful, life-giving word of *Christ* called out, "Lazarus, come forth" (John 11:43), it enabled him to respond. Then he "came forth, bound hand and foot with wrappings" (John 11:44). Man's free will is bound and constrained by his own sin. Therefore, salvation is impossible apart from God's sovereign, predestinating grace.

---

[3] Roger S. Greenway, "Calvinism," in A. Scott Moreau, ed., *Evangelical Dictionary of World Missions* (Grand Rapids: Baker, 2000), 156.

In fact, Jesus declares God's sovereignty while simultaneously inviting sinners to come.

> All that the Father gives Me shall come to Me [sovereignty], and the one who comes to Me I will certainly not cast out [free offer]. (John 6:37)

> And this is the will of Him who sent Me, that of all that He has given Me I lose nothing, but raise it up on the last day. For this is the will of My Father, that everyone who beholds the Son and believes in Him, may have eternal life; and I Myself will raise him up on the last day. (John 6:39–40)

So then, unless God gives men to Christ they will not come. Thus, the Bible sees no conflict between God's sovereignty and his free offer of the gospel.

When Paul is preaching in Pisidian Antioch, he declares God's good news of salvation to all who will hear it, both Jew and Greek (Acts 13:32, 38, 46). But when Luke records the *results* of Paul's preaching, he writes as one who understands the free-offer of the gospel will only be received by the elect:

> And Paul and Barnabas spoke out boldly and said, 'It was necessary that the word of God should be spoken to you first; since you repudiate it, and judge yourselves unworthy of eternal life, behold, we are turning to the Gentiles. . . .' And when the Gentiles heard this, they began rejoicing and glorifying the word of the Lord; and as many as had been appointed to eternal life believed. (Acts 13:46, 48)

We also see Luke's explanation of the sovereign grace of God with Lydia. "And a certain woman named Lydia, from the city of Thyatira, a seller of purple fabrics, a worshiper of God, was listening; and *the Lord opened her heart* [sovereignty] *to respond* [free will] to the things spoken by Paul [free offer]" (Acts 16:14). Christ himself notes that only his sheep will follow him: "My sheep hear My voice, and I know them, and they follow Me; and I give eternal life to them, and they shall never perish; and no one shall snatch them out of My hand" (John 10:27–28). The non-elect will not come to follow him, for they are not his "sheep" (John 10:26). This is because God "gavest Him authority over all mankind, that *to all whom Thou hast given Him*, He may give eternal life" (John 17:2).

These texts demand that we understand that unless God gives sinners to Christ they will not come. God's sovereignty makes the free offer of the gospel effective. The free offer goes out to all, but only the elect will respond. "Many are called, but few are chosen" (Matt 22:14).

"Predestination discourages motives to exertion"

Many surmise a certain debilitating logic to predestination: "If predestination is true then what is the point of evangelizing? After all, if God sovereignly predestines those who will be saved from before the foundation of the world, why should we worry ourselves with personally witnessing to others? There is nothing we can do about it, since it has been predestined."

This objection can go further: "What is the point of praying for people's salvation? Or preaching the gospel?" Or sending out missionaries? God will get his will done without our help." In fact, an extreme application of this line of thinking apart from the question of salvation is to ask: "Why should we get an education, seek a job, look for a wife, or any number of human actions, since God has predestined whatsoever comes to pass irrespective of any human self-determination?"

We should note that there is, in fact, a perversion of biblical predestination which develops along these lines (just as perversions encumber any number of theological truths). It is known as Hyper-Calvinism. Hyper-Calvinists actually believe it is wrong to evangelize, to offer the gospel to sinners, and to send out missionaries. They believe that this is contrary to the will of God and is an act of arrogance on the part of man. This view has only been held by a small minority of Calvinists and is roundly criticized by the majority. Hyper-Calvinism is expressed in Articles 26 and 33 of the *Articles of Faith of the Gospel Standard Aid and Poor Relief Societies* (1878) where we read:

> We deny duty faith and duty repentance — these terms suggesting that it is every man's duty spiritually and savingly to repent and believe. . . . We reject the doctrine that man in a state of nature should be exhorted to believe in or turn to God. (Article 26)

> Therefore, that for ministers in the present day to address unconverted persons, or indiscriminately all in a mixed congregation, calling upon them to savingly repent, believe, and receive Christ, or perform any other acts dependent upon the new creative power of the Holy Ghost, is, on the one hand, to imply creature power, and on the other, to deny the doctrine of special redemption. (Article 33)

How shall we respond to such troubling objections?"

First, such objections are not limited to the matter of predestination. We must always be careful to think through our objections to various biblical doctrines. The biblical revelation is a seamless garment with all the various doctrines forming a unified, coherent truth. If we are not careful, we can attack one doctrine and take others down with it.

For instance, do we not have promises of God in Scripture that specifically pledge us God's blessings apart from any and all self-effort?

> For this reason I say to you, do not be anxious for your life, as to what you shall eat, or what you shall drink; nor for your body, as to what you shall put on. Is not life more than food, and the body than clothing? . . . Do not be anxious then, saying, "What shall we eat?" or "What shall we drink?" or "With what shall we clothe ourselves?" For all these things the Gentiles eagerly seek; for

your heavenly Father knows that you need all these things. (Matt 6:25, 31–32)

In fact, did not Christ himself teach us to simply pray and ask God for our food? "Give us this day our daily bread" (Matt 6:11). If predestination to salvation implies that we need not labor in the gospel, then the Lord's prayer implies that we should not labor for food! But we intrinsically know that this is a misinterpretation and misapplication of Scripture. After all, Paul writes: "If anyone will not work, neither let him eat" (2 Thess 3:10).

And what about the glorious promise of prayer? "Ask, and it shall be given to you; seek, and you shall find; knock, and it shall be opened to you. . . . If you then, being evil, know how to give good gifts to your children, how much more shall your Father who is in heaven give what is good to those who ask Him!" (Matt 7:1, 7). Does this imply that we should merely pray for everything we need and God will give it to us, so that to work for such is a sign of a lack of faith?

Second, such objections overlook the fact that predestination involves not only the end but also the means to the end. That is, a biblical doctrine of predestination is comprehensive, for "he works *all* things after the counsel of his own will" (Eph 1:11). This demands that he not only predestine that a particular person be saved, but also *how* that person is saved. Such God-ordained means include personal prayer, studying the gospel message, diligent gospel proclamation, and many other factors.

As Loraine Boettner expressed it:

It is not merely a few isolated events here and there that have been foreordained, but the whole chain of events, with all of their inter-relations and connections.. All of the parts form a unit in the Divine plan. . . . If God has purposed that a man shall reap, He has also purposed that he shall sow.[4]

Thus we cannot say: "God predestined something, therefore I do not have to do anything." This denies the doctrine of predestination *as revealed in the Bible*, a comprehensive doctrine that involves means as well as ends. Christ also commands: "*seek* and ye *shall* find"; he does not teach us: "Sit and it shall come your way." If God did not ordain the means to the end, then we are fatalists. Fatalism involves impersonal inevitability and the bypassing of means.

As Martin Luther amusingly put it: "The farmer who, after hearing a sermon on God's decrees, took the breakneck road instead of the safe one to his home and broke his wagon in consequence, concludes before the end of the journey that he at any rate had been predestinated to be a fool, and that he had made his calling and election sure."[5]

Third, such objections contradict the true practical consequences of the doctrine. If we truly believe that God sovereignly controls all things, then we should be *more earnest* in our prayers and *more diligent* in our spiritual and material labors. For we know that "if God be for us, who can be against us?" (Rom 8:31). And we know that the will of God revealed in Scripture commands us to pray, evangelize, labor, and so forth.

---

[4] Boettner, *The Reformed Doctrine of Predestination*, 254.

[5] Martin Luther, *The Bondage of the Will*, as cited in Boettner, *Reformed Doctrine of Predestination*, 256.

Chapter 9
APPLYING THE DOCTRINE

God has revealed the various doctrines of Scripture so that we might be spiritually strengthened in understanding his will, ways, and world. All biblical doctrines have a practical impact on our understanding, worshiping, obeying, and serving God. God's providence and sovereignty are not simply esoteric, abstract doctrines interesting only to those with theological or philosophical inclinations. They are not mind-games or puzzles for our amusement. When properly understood, they necessarily have a practical impact upon our lives in many respects. Doctrine is given to practically transform us, as we can see from the following references:

> You shall know the truth, and the truth shall make you free. (John 8:32)

> All Scripture is inspired by God and profitable for teaching, for reproof, for correction, for training in righteousness; that the man of God may be adequate, equipped for every good work. (2 Tim 3:16–17)

> For though by this time you ought to be teachers, you have need again for someone to teach you the elementary principles of the oracles of God, and you have come to need milk and not solid food. For everyone who partakes only of milk is not accustomed to the word of righteousness, for he is a babe. But solid food is for the mature, who because of practice have their senses trained to discern good and evil. (Heb 5:12–14)

> Therefore, putting aside all malice and all guile and hypocrisy and envy and all slander, like newborn babes, long for the pure milk of the word, that by it you may grow in respect to salvation. (1 Pet 2:1–2)

In that God's word is designed to exercise a practical impact on our lives, we need to consider some of the positive implications of affirming his absolute sovereignty in predestination. Let us begin by considering:

Sovereignty Provides Your Salvation

The doctrine of sovereignty teaches that God chooses you for salvation from *before* the foundation of the world. Election is based on God's own sovereign and mysterious will, not on the foreseen conditions or actions of man. God's election makes salvation *totally* gracious, secured *solely* by the undeserved, merciful love of God.

> All that the Father *gives Me* will come to Me, and the one who comes to Me I will by no means cast out. (John 6:37)

> Jesus spoke these words, lifted up His eyes to heaven, and said: "Father, the hour has come. Glorify Your Son, that Your Son also may glorify You, as You have given Him authority over all flesh, that *He should give eternal life to as many as You have given Him*." (John 17:1–2)

> Now when the Gentiles heard this, they were glad and glorified the word of the Lord. And *as many as had been appointed to eternal life believed*. (Acts 13:48)

> Blessed be the God and Father of our Lord Jesus Christ, who has blessed us with every spiritual blessing in the heavenly places in Christ, [4] just as *He chose us in Him before the foundation of the world*, that we should be holy and without blame before Him in love. (Eph 1:3–4)

> In Him also we have obtained an inheritance, *being predestined according to the purpose of Him who works all things according to the counsel of His will*. (Eph 1:11)

> He has saved us and called us with a holy calling, *not according to our works, but according to His own purpose and grace which was given to us in Christ Jesus before time began*. (2 Tim 1:9)

Sovereignty Insures Your Security

God's sovereignty is the basis for assurance of your salvation. Your very security in Christ depends on God's sovereign will, and on nothing else. Because of God's sovereignty nothing can cause you to fall from your ultimate salvation. Your salvation does not depend upon your own self-effort or inherent goodness, but on God's almighty, saving, free grace. Nothing can cause you to fall from your ultimate eternal salvation.

> And this is the Father's will which hath sent me, that of all which he hath *given* me I should lose nothing, but should raise it up again at the last day. (John 6:39)

> No man can come to me, except the Father which hath sent me draw him: and I will raise him up at the last day. (John 6:44)

> My sheep hear My voice, and I know them, and they follow Me; and I give eternal life to them, and they shall never perish; and no one shall snatch them out of My hand. My Father, who has given them to Me, is greater than all; and *no one is able to snatch them out of the Father's hand.* (John 10:27–29)

> And we know that *God causes* all things to work together for good to those who love God, to those who are called *according to His purpose.* (Rom 8:28)

> We have obtained an inheritance, having been *predestined* according to *His purpose* who works all things after *the counsel of His will.* (Eph 1:11)

Calvin writes: "We shall never be clearly persuaded, as we ought to be, that our salvation flows from the wellspring of God's free mercy until we come to know his eternal election, which illumines God's grace by this contrast: that he does not indiscriminately adopt all into the hope of salvation but gives to some what he denies to others."[1]

Sovereignty Lessens Your Sorrow

Since understanding God's sovereignty provides you with security, it becomes a source of comfort encouraging you even during trials, comforting you while enduring affliction. This doctrine teaches that God is particularly concerned with you and the details of your life. You do not live in a random world, but one controlled by God for his own glorious ends. You provide no comfort if you tell someone suffering: "Satan did this; God never would." Or: "God has been thwarted in his good intentions for you." The Bible directs you to recognize the hand of God at work in your life, even when in affliction.

> And as for you, you meant evil against me, but God meant it for good in order to bring about this present result, to preserve many people alive. (Gen 50:20)

> And he said, "Naked I came from my mother's womb, And naked I shall return there. / The Lord gave and the Lord has taken away. Blessed be the name of the Lord." (Job 1:21)

> And do not fear those who kill the body, but are unable to kill the soul; but rather fear Him who is able to destroy both soul and body in hell. Are not two sparrows sold for a cent? And yet not one of them will fall to the ground apart from your Father. But the very hairs of your head are all numbered. Therefore do not fear; you are of more value than many sparrows. (Matt 10:28–31)

> And we know that God causes all things to work together for good to those who love God, to those who are called according to His purpose. (Rom 8:28)

---

[1] Cited in Lillback, *The Binding of God*, 214.

And in nothing terrified by your adversaries: which is to them an evident token of perdition, but to you of salvation, and that of God. For unto you it is given in the behalf of Christ, not only to believe on him, but also to suffer for his sake. (Phil 1:28–29)

For the which cause I also suffer these things: nevertheless I am not ashamed: for I know whom I have believed, and am persuaded that he is able to keep that which I have committed unto him against that day. (2 Tim 1:12)

Humble yourselves, therefore, under the mighty hand of God, that He may exalt you at the proper time, casting all your anxiety upon Him, because He cares for you. (1 Pet 5:6)

This comfort is well captured in the gospel hymn: "Known Only to Him," which has one stanza that declares: "I know not what the future holds, / But I know who holds the future."

Sovereignty Deepens Your Humility

A clear apprehension of God's sovereignty humbles you before God. If God is sovereignly at work throughout the world, then you are absolutely dependent upon him. God saves you, not you yourself. A conviction of this truth removes all temptation to pride in yourself.

Now, therefore, it was not you who sent me here, but God; and He has made me a father to Pharaoh and lord of all his household and ruler over all the land of Egypt. (Gen 45:8)

You did not choose Me, but I chose you, and appointed you, that you should go and bear fruit, and that your fruit should remain, that whatever you ask of the Father in My name, He may give to you. (John 15:16)

For who regards you as superior? And what do you have that you did not receive? But if you did receive it, why do you boast as if you had not received it? (1 Cor 4:7)

He has saved us, and called us with a holy calling, not according to our works, but according to His own purpose and grace which was granted us in Christ Jesus from all eternity. (2 Tim 1:9)

Come now, you who say, "Today or tomorrow, we shall go to such and such a city, and spend a year there and engage in business and make a profit." Yet you do not know what your life will be like tomorrow. You are just a vapor that appears for a little while and then vanishes away. Instead, you ought to say, "If the Lord wills, we shall live and also do this or that." But as it is, you boast in your arrogance; all such boasting is evil. (Jms 4:13–16)

Humble yourselves, therefore, under the mighty hand of God, that He may exalt you at the proper time, casting all your anxiety upon Him, because He cares for you. (1 Pet 5:6–7)

After you have suffered for a little while, the God of all grace, who called you to His eternal glory in Christ, will Himself perfect, confirm, strengthen and establish you. To Him be dominion forever and ever. Amen. (1 Pet 5:10–11)

Sovereignty Exalts God's Majesty

God's absolute sovereignty brings all glory to him as the majestic sovereign over all the Universe. In fact, God exercises it for that very purpose.

Wherefore, accept one another, just as Christ also accepted us to the glory of God. (Rom 15:7)

He predestined us to adoption as sons through Jesus Christ to Himself, according to the kind intention of His will, to the praise of the glory of His grace, which He freely bestowed on us in the Beloved. In Him we have redemption through His blood, the forgiveness of our trespasses, according to the riches of His grace. (Eph 1:5–7)

We have obtained an inheritance, having been predestined according to His purpose who works all things after the counsel of His will, to the end that we who were the first to hope in Christ should be to the praise of His glory. (Eph 1:11–12)

My God shall supply all your needs according to His riches in glory in Christ Jesus. Now to our God and Father be the glory forever and ever. Amen. (Phil 4:19–20)

Whoever speaks, let him speak, as it were, the utterances of God; whoever serves, let him do so as by the strength which God supplies; so that in all things God may be glorified through Jesus Christ, to whom belongs the glory and dominion forever and ever. Amen. (1 Pet 4:11)

Worthy are You, our Lord and our God, to receive glory and honor and power; for You created all things, and because of Your will they existed, and were created. (Rev 4:11)

We started our study of predestination with this comment: "Undoubtedly, predestination is one of the most daunting, demanding, and debated doctrines in Scripture." Due to this reality, the question arises:

Why Study Predestination?

Too often, Christians who are perplexed by the doctrine of predestination will ask why we should bother studying such a confusing and debated doctrine. A number of reasons compel us to study this issue.

First, the Bible does, in fact, teach the doctrine. In Scripture we frequently discover the words "predestine/predestination" (Acts 4:28; Rom 8:29–30; 1 Cor 2:7; Eph 1:5, 11), "elect/election" (Matt 24:22, 24, 31; Mark 13:20; 22, 27; Luke 18:7; Rom 8:33), and related terms ("chosen," "called," etc.). And we know that "all Scripture is profitable" (2 Tim 3:16). In fact, Jesus prays: "sanctify them through Your truth; Your word is truth" (John 17:17) and Paul states that whatever is written is "for our instruction" (Rom 15:4).

Second, Christians should want to know the "whole counsel of God" (Acts 20:27). After all, we are to live by "every word" that proceeds out of the mouth of God (Deut 8:3). God has given us his word that we might better know him and more fully trust him. Therefore, we must be "constantly nourished on the words of the faith and of the sound doctrine" in Scripture (1 Tim 4:6). Why would we *not* want to know teachings about our God? How can we think certain biblical stated doctrines are expendable?

Third, this doctrine is designed to bring glory to God. Paul teaches us that "He chose us in Him before the foundation of the world, that we should be holy and blameless before Him. In love He predestined us to adoption as sons through Jesus Christ to Himself, according to the kind intention of His will, *to the praise of the glory of His grace*, which He freely bestowed on us in the Beloved" (Eph 1:4–6).

Fourth, God expects us to defend his word and will in the world. As a general rule we ought as Christians to "be ready to make a defense to everyone who asks" of us (1 Pet 3:15). Predestination appears in Scripture; we must respond to those who would attack it in that we must "know how to respond to each person" (Col 4:6). Paul illustrates this for us in Romans 9 where he even brings up the questions that men ask, so that he can answer them in his instructional letter to all the Christians in Rome: "You will say to me then, 'Why does He still find fault? For who resists His will?'" (Rom 9:19).

Differences of Opinion

Conservative, evangelical Christians all agree that not all men will be saved. Historic Christianity is not universalistic. So we must ask then: What makes the difference between the saved and the lost? Why are some saved and others lost? The answers to these types of questions sort out the major evangelical positions.

Lutheranism.[1] Lutherans teach that certain men are saved because they do not resist God's grace. Grace is offered to all men, but indwelling sin leads many to resist God's free offer of the gospel.

---

[1] Lutheranism is the branch of Christianity which arose from the teachings of Martin Luther (1483–1546). Ironically, modern Lutheranism generally does not follow the strong predestinarian views of Luther himself.

Arminianism.[2] Arminians believe that man must cooperate with God's grace in order to be saved. Though man is a sinner, he is not totally depraved. Consequently, he has a latent ability to do good and to accept God's offer.

Calvinism.[3] Calvinists believe that man is a sinner who is depraved in every part of his being so that he is unable and unwilling to reach out to God. Therefore, God must save man by sovereignly opening his heart and giving him new life, so that he may believe in Christ.

By now we should see that four leading problems face the non-Calvinistic approaches to salvation.

First, non-Calvinists do not understand the seriousness of man's sinful condition. Yet Scripture teaches that it is so serious that it precludes man from doing anything worthy and acceptable in the eyes of God. The doctrine of Total Depravity teaches that sin affects *every* aspect of man's being (body, soul, mind, will, emotions, intellect, etc.). Total Depravity does not imply that man is as evil as he can be (God's common grace prevents the absolute dominance of sin). Because of man's inherent depravity, though, he is wholly unable and unwilling even to savingly believe the gospel or to please God.

The Scriptures plainly declare that man's sin absolutely incapacitates him in this regard:

> Can the Ethiopian change his skin / Or the leopard his spots? / Then you also can do good / Who are accustomed to doing evil. (Jer 13:23)

---

[2] This terms is derived from the name of James (or Jacobus) Arminius (1560 –1609). He was a Dutch theologian who resisted the Calvinistic theology so widely prevalent in Holland in his day.

[3] This term is derived from the name of the leading Reformer, John Calvin (1509–64). The famed French theologian strongly emphasized the absolute sovereignty of God in his system of belief.

And this is the judgment, that the light is come into the world, and *men loved the darkness rather than the light*; for their deeds were evil. (John 3:19)

No one can come to Me, unless the Father who sent Me draws him; and I will raise him up on the last day. (John 6:44)

For this reason I have said to you, that *no one can come to Me*, unless it has been granted him from the Father. (John 6:65)

The mind set on the flesh is hostile toward God; for it does not subject itself to the law of God, for *it is not even able* to do so; and those who are in the flesh *cannot please God*. (Rom 8:7–8)

And you were *dead* in your trespasses and sins. (Eph 2:1; cp. Col 2:13)

Second, non-Calvinists credit man with some aspect of his own salvation. The sinner's response — the consent of man's fallen, corrupt, rebellious will — is the determining act that brings salvation to one individual, while another individual rejects it. This contradicts the following passages of Scripture:

As many as received Him, to them He gave the right to become children of God, even to those who believe in His name, *who were born not of blood, nor of the will of the flesh, nor of the will of man, but of God*. (John 1:12–13)

And a certain woman named Lydia, from the city of Thyatira, a seller of purple fabrics, a worshiper of God, was listening; and *the Lord opened her heart* to respond to the things spoken by Paul. (Acts 16:14)

For by grace you have been saved through faith; and that *not of yourselves*, it is the *gift of God*; *not* as a result of *works*, that no one should boast. (Eph 2:8–9)

For to you *it has been granted* for Christ's sake, not only *to believe in Him*, but also to suffer for His sake. (Phil 1:29)

> Perhaps *God may grant them repentance* leading to the knowledge
> of the truth, and they may come to their senses and escape from
> the snare of the devil, having been held captive by him to do his
> will. (2 Tim 2:25–26)

Third, non-Calvinists inadvertently teach that lost men illustrate
God's failure. This results because they believe that God's decree
opens the door of salvation to all men, the work of the Holy Spirit
works equally among all men, and the death of Christ applies uni-
versally to all. Yet despite all of this, the majority of men are lost.

> So shall My word be which goes forth from My mouth. It shall not
> return to Me empty without accomplishing what I desire, and
> without succeeding in the matter for which I sent it. (Isa 55:11)

> All the inhabitants of the earth are accounted as nothing. He
> does according to His will in the host of heaven and among the
> inhabitants of earth. No one can ward off His hand or say to Him,
> 'What hast Thou done?' (Dan 4:35)

> Do not marvel that I said to you, "You must be born again." The
> wind blows where it wishes and you hear the sound of it, but do
> not know where it comes from and where it is going; so is
> everyone who is born of the Spirit. (John 3:7–8)

> All that the Father gives Me shall come to Me, and the one who
> comes to Me I will certainly not cast out. (John 6:37)

> Knowing, brethren beloved by God, His choice of you; for our
> gospel did not come to you in word only, but also in power and
> in the Holy Spirit and with full conviction; just as you know what
> kind of men we proved to be among you for your sake. (1 Thess
> 1:4–5)

Fourth, non-Calvinists effectively deny that God's grace actually
saves anyone. It only provides the *opportunity* for saving all men
rather than the *certainty* of saving any. Charles Spurgeon once illus-
trated this by saying the non-Calvinist view of salvation presents us
with a great wide bridge that goes across the River Jordan — but

only half way, then it stops. Whereas the Calvinist view is of a narrow bridge which goes all the way across. The saving work of Christ is not merely hypothetical, rather it is actual; it is not partially but fully redemptive.

> For just as the Father raises the dead and gives them life, even so *the Son also gives life* to whom He wishes. (John 5:21)

> I am the good shepherd; and I know My own, and My own know Me, even as the Father knows Me and I know the Father; and I lay down My life for the sheep. (John 10:14–15)

> For if while we were enemies, we were *reconciled to God through the death of His Son*, much more, having been reconciled, we shall be *saved by His life*. (Rom 5:10)

> *Christ redeemed us* from the curse of the Law, having become a curse for us — for it is written, 'Cursed is everyone who hangs on a tree.' (Gal 3:13)

> Husbands, love your wives, just as Christ also loved the church and gave Himself up for her; that He might sanctify her, having cleansed her by the washing of water with the word. (Eph 5:25–26)

> For He delivered us from the domain of darkness, and transferred us to the kingdom of His beloved Son, in whom we have redemption, the forgiveness of sins. (Col 1:13–14)

> And although you were formerly alienated and hostile in mind, engaged in evil deeds, yet He has now reconciled you in His fleshly body through death, in order to present you before Him holy and blameless and beyond reproach. (Col 1:21–22)

> It is a trustworthy statement, deserving full acceptance, that Christ Jesus came into the world to save sinners, among whom I am foremost of all. (1 Tim 1:15)

He gave Himself for us, that He might redeem us from every lawless deed and purify for Himself a people for His own possession, zealous for good deeds. (Tit 2:14)

And from Jesus Christ, the faithful witness, the first-born of the dead, and the ruler of the kings of the earth. To Him who loves us, and released us from our sins by His blood, and He has made us to be a kingdom, priests to His God and Father; to Him be the glory and the dominion forever and ever. Amen. (Rev 1:5–6)

And all who dwell on the earth will worship him, everyone whose name has not been *written from the foundation of the world in the book of life of the Lamb* who has been slain. (Rev 13:8)

Final Exhortation

Predestination may be "the most daunting, demanding, and debated doctrine in Scripture," but it *is* a doctrine *in* Scripture. And as Peter recognized, Scripture has "some things hard to understand" (2 Pet 3:15–16). Nevertheless, "all Scripture is inspired by God and profitable for teaching, for reproof, for correction, for training in righteousness; that the man of God may be adequate, equipped for every good work" (2 Tim 3:16–17). Therefore, you should "be diligent to present yourself approved to God as a workman who does not need to be ashamed, handling accurately the word of truth" (2 Tim 2:15) — even regarding this difficult doctrine.

www.ingramcontent.com/pod-product-compliance
Lightning Source LLC
Chambersburg PA
CBHW060348090426
42734CB00011B/2075